Do Not Give Up!

Do Not Give Up!

Bosede Apata MSN, FNP-C, PMHNP-BC

Published by:
Dewalette Creations LLC
dewalette@gmail.com

Copyright © 2021 by Bosede Apata
First Edition

Softcover ISBN: 978-1-7371861-0-6
Ebook ISBN: 978-1-7371861-1-3

For more information, contact author:
Email: peacefulheart.joy@gmail.com

CONTENTS

DEDICATION

This book is dedicated to God's children ALL over the world to encourage us not to grow weary on our "wilderness journeys." It is dedicated to the weak, tired, frustrated, abused, miserable, heartbroken, hopeless, discouraged and someone planning to throw in the towel. In addition, the "strong" can benefit from it as a prophylactic therapy because it is written: *"Therefore let him who thinks he stands take heed lest he fall"* (1 Corinthians 10:12 NKJV). This book is All About Holistic Minds (AAHM). My prayer is that it will touch souls, bodies and minds in the mighty name of Jesus.

May the good Lord continue to uphold all of us with His right hand of righteousness and keep us from falling or given up, in the name of Jesus. May we remain firm and immovable in the Lord, and may our lamps keep burning bright as we wait patiently for the coming of our Lord, in the mighty name of Jesus. Amen!

GRATITUDE

I am incredibly grateful to God for the opportunity and inspiration given me to write this book. I thank Him for the "schools" of different life experiences He has sent me to be able to know that the ONLY way out is Jesus! He has been and will continue to be my help, teacher, comforter and my ALL in ALL. I thank Him for my mountains, my valleys and the storms He brought me through. I worship Him for my "wilderness journey."

I praise His holy name for the opened and closed doors, for my successes and failures. I am grateful for the friends who left me and the ones who stood by me. I cannot thank God enough for the "Judases" and the amazing "Jonathans" in my life. How can I forget the "Hamans," who are yet to hang themselves on their own "gallows," unless they repent? For my "Peninnahs," who had fun mocking me for many years, I am very grateful! Your attitudes, harsh words, disrespect, ridicule, rejections and all that God allowed me to pass through in your hands were ORDAINED by Him. You all have encouraged me to cry unto my God in agony, and He has answered me. Hallelujah! God knows that I am NOT holding anything against you. He has helped me to forgive you all. I had already given my heart to the "heart mender" before coming across the "heart breakers." He has been faithful; He guarded my heart and did NOT allow the enemy to break it beyond repair. I am praying for "spiritual amnesia" because; I don't even want to remember any of the wrongdoing ANYMORE, in the name of Jesus. My prayer is: *"Create in me a clean heart, O God, and renew a steadfast spirit within me"* (Psalm 51:10 NKJV). All of you are cordially invited to celebrate God's given "Samuel" with me. *"This was the LORD's doing; It is marvelous in our eyes"* (Psalm 118:23 NKJV). If you did not do all you did to me, I would have been too comfortable and may not have seen the need to forge ahead. God has used you to help me be ALL that He wants me to be, to His glory, honor and adoration! From the bottom of my heart, I say, THANK YOU VERY MUCH FOR EVERYTHING! Kindly forgive me if I have wronged you in any way as well.

I want to say a big THANK YOU to my spiritual leaders, those who took it upon themselves to intercede on my behalf. Your intercessory prayers have been answered; the "chains" are broken, in the name of Jesus. May the blessings of God continue to be upon you and all yours, in the mighty name of Jesus. Amen! It is written: *"I will bless those who bless you, and I will curse him who curses you; and in you, all the families of the earth shall be blessed"* (Genesis 12:3 NKJV). I am indeed very grateful. May the good Lord bless you in all your endeavors, may He grant you all your heart's desires, according to His will, in the mighty name of Jesus. Amen!

To my amazing professors, preceptors/mentors, who guided and supported me through my career, I am very grateful for the seeds you have sown in me through the help of God. Thank you for allowing God to use you. May God bless you and all yours, in the name of Jesus. Amen

Special thanks to my darling husband, Dr. Olusegun Apata, for all you have done, all you are doing and all you will do through the help of God. May God continue to bless you, in the name of Jesus. Amen! Thank you very much, dear. I love you. To my beautiful, loving and caring children: Markell and Tinu Dorsainvil, Andrew and Tomi Adeniyi, Tolu, Toba Apata, I can't thank you enough for standing by me and all the support you gave me. I praise the name of God for blessing me with beautiful grandchildren: Ayla (Morayo), Elijah (Adewale), Malcolm (Adeyemi) and Shiloh (Adekemi). I love you all. Everyone has played salient roles that have encouraged me to want to motivate other people and remind them that God is in TOTAL control of all our lives and that He has a reason for making us go through WHATEVER we are passing through now, what we may pass through in the future or what we have already passed through, as we travel along our "wilderness journeys."

I just want to say: DO NOT GIVE UP! By the grace of God, it is going to be a very happy and glorious ending, and the name of God will be FOREVER praised, in the name of Jesus. Amen! It is written: *"And we know that all things work together for good to those who love God, to those who are the called according to His purpose"* (Romans 8:28 NKJV). Do not give up on God because He will not give up on you. HE LOVES YOU!

DECLARATION

I want to declare that the songs in this book are not mine, but they have helped me tremendously in my "wilderness journey," and I pray they bless and revive your soul, as well, in the name of Jesus. Many thanks to the music artistes and songwriters; I wish you more anointing and divine inspiration in the name of Jesus. Moreover, relevant hymns are applied as needed.

I love to sing or make my "joyful noise" unto my God. I found singing very therapeutic during my "wilderness journey." I have been inspired to write some songs as well (mostly in Yoruba). They are available on CD Baby and iTunes. I am using English songs from other artistes for the benefit of those who don't speak Yoruba. I know and appreciate the importance of music in mental health. So, don't be surprised to see a list of songs as you read. When you are feeling down, and a song comes to your mind, the emotional, physical, mental and other negative feelings may stand in the way at first, and you may not be able to praise as you want to. I want to testify that once God grants you the courage to start the praise song (even if you have to cry as you sing), I promise you will feel a lot better as you sing along and meditate on the words of the song. Sing in the shower, it is good for your lungs. In the house, when cleaning, it will give you strength. Have a song in your heart and meditate on it when you cannot sing it aloud; at work, anywhere and anytime as long as you do not disturb others and it is not affecting your concentration and productivity. The Lord is moved when we praise Him. He will destroy the plans of the enemy and deliver you, in the name of Jesus. Amen! If you love to dance like me, it will even make you feel much better. I call it a "spiritual workout." It will bless you spiritually, emotionally, mentally and physically. So, darling brother/sister in the Lord, it is time to sing, meditate and dance away your sorrow, in the mighty name of Jesus. Amen!

BIOGRAPHY

Bosede is the fourth child of Pastor J.A. Adeniji and late Mrs. A.A. Adeniji. She is a board-certified family nurse practitioner. She started her nursing career as a licensed practical nurse (LPN). She received her LPN training from; Lake Michigan College, Benton Harbor, Michigan and bachelor's degree in nursing (BSN) from Indiana University Northwest, Gary, Indiana. She obtained her master's degree in nursing (MSN, FNP) from Governors State University, University Park, Illinois. Recently, she completed a certification program in psychiatry, mental health nurse practitioner from the University of Texas, Rio Grande Valley. To the glory of God, she is a board-certified psychiatric mental health nurse practitioner. Hallelujah! She prays for the grace to be able to join other providers in fighting the shortage of mental health care providers, with the goal of making a positive influence in the lives of the patients God will send her way. Bosede is very loving, caring and compassionate to all. She has a special place in her heart for the elderly, mentally/emotionally challenged, abused and terminally ill/dying patients, a passion she demonstrated through her work in skilled nursing facilities, behavioral, palliative/hospice, medical, surgical and telemetry units.

Furthermore, Bosede acknowledges that she is a sinner, interested in "hanging out" with other sinners, willing to let them know that we have been saved by grace. NOTHING, but God's grace (Ephesians 2:8-9). She wants to remind others that the blood of Jesus has washed our sins away (Colossians 1:20, Hebrews 9:14, Ephesians 1:7, Hebrews 13:12 and Leviticus 17:11). Don't let your past sins stand in the way of you enjoying the grace of God. Moreover, Bosede wants to remind others that we are qualified to be called children of God (Romans 8:16, John 1:12, 2 Corinthians 6:18 and Galatians 3:26). Furthermore, feelings of rejection, discrimination, prejudice and inferiority/superiority complexes are destroyed because we are children of the most high, God. It is very crucial for us to know that our names and titles have changed; We are princes/princesses because our Father is the King of kings, Lord of lords, everlasting Father and the Prince of Peace (Isaiah 9:6). HALLELUYAH!

MOTIVATIONAL WORDS FOR READERS

My brother/sister in the Lord, I am writing this through the inspiration of the lifter of my/your head (ALMIGHTY GOD), for us to keep our heads up high. You might have been fooled or lied to, disappointed, betrayed, rejected or abandoned. You might have been told that you will never amount to anything in life. All these negative pronunciations are from the agents of the enemy. They are not from the Lord. The world may not see the glory of God in you YET, but at God's own APPOINTED time, you will be reintroduced and be celebrated accordingly, in the name of Jesus. Amen! Do not listen to the lies of the enemy. Ignore the ridicule or anything the enemy wants to use to break you. Instead, allow God to use them to build you. May God grant all of us the grace to get BETTER and not bitter as we go through this "wilderness journey" called life, in the name of Jesus. It may seem like you are in the "oven" right now due to the "heat" of life you are experiencing or that you have experienced. By the grace of God, you are going to come out "WELL DONE," in the mighty name of Jesus. Amen!

It may seem so dark all around you now that you can't even see anything. Don't panic; the Lord is with you, guiding your steps, and He will not let you fall. Remind yourself that YOU ARE NEVER ALONE! HALLELUJAH! Do not let the enemy stop you from praying and praising God, even in the dark seasons of life. The Lord will pave the way for you, in the name of Jesus. May God grant you the divine "earplugs" to block the environmental noise that may be distracting you from hearing Him clearly. Darling brother/sister in the Lord, hold on tight; morning is coming!

"For His anger is but for a moment, His favor is for life; Weeping may endure for a night, but joy comes in the morning" (Psalm 30:5 NKJV).

Your "Friday" may be filled with a lot of pain. You may be saying to yourself, "How long, Father?" It is becoming too long and unbearable, and you are desperately in need of a quick solution. I plead with you to let God work it out for you, in His own way and at the appropriate time. Please, do not give up, darling brother/sister. "Sunday" is coming, and it is going to be **GLORIOUS**, in the mighty name of Jesus. Amen!

Your story is not going to end the way it is now. You are not going to die in the "sweat"; continue to trust in the Lord because "sweet" is around the corner, about to be served, and you are going to enjoy every bit of it, in sound health, joy and peace of mind, in the name of Jesus. Amen! The ones who have given up on you will soon come and rejoice with you. Those who have been looking down on you will soon look up to you, in the mighty name of Jesus. Amen!

"When my father and my mother forsake me, then the Lord will take care of me" (Psalm 27:10 NKJV).

"And it shall come to pass in the place where it was said to them, you are not my people, there they shall be called sons of the living God" (Romans 9:26 NKJV).

You may be feeling knocked down, thinking this is the end. Darling child of God, you will NEVER be "knocked out." The Good Lord will pick you up, and you will NEVER fall again, in the name of Jesus. Amen! It is written: *"For a righteous man may fall seven times and rise again, but the wicked shall fall by calamity"* (Proverbs 24:16 NKJV).

"The steps of a good man are ordered by the Lord, and He delights in his way. Though he falls, he shall not be utterly cast down; For the Lord upholds him with His hand"
(Psalm 37:23-24 NKJV).

The blessings may be delayed, but you will NEVER be denied of ANYTHING God has promised you. Be patient, continue to trust in the Lord. He is FAITHFUL, and He will deliver, AT HIS OWN TIME, in the name of Jesus. Amen!

"He has made everything beautiful in its time. Also, He has put eternity in their hearts, except that no one can find out the work that God does from beginning to end" (Ecclesiastes 3:11 NKJV).

"Therefore know that the Lord your God, He is God, the faithful God who keeps covenant and mercy for a thousand generations

with those who love Him and keep His commandments" (Deuteronomy 7:9 NKJV).

God is taking you through these bumpy and rough roads for a reason. Everything will end up in victory, in the mighty name of Jesus. Amen! You are going to testify, and your testimony will bring souls to God. Your song of victory will soon be: "I didn't know, you will honor/favor me this way, Lord!" May the good Lord surprise you beyond your imagination, in the mighty name of Jesus. Amen! **DO NOT GIVE UP!**

Song of Meditation "I Didn't Know You Will Honor Me This Way, Lord"
(Nigerian Praise Song)!

I didn't know you will honor me this way Lord.
I didn't know you will honor me this way Baba.
I didn't know you will honor me this way.
Honor me this way, thank you Jesus.
I didn't know you will favor me this way Lord.
I didn't know you will favor me this way Baba.
I didn't know you will favor me this way.
Favor me this way. Thank you, Jesus.

I have a Father who will never, never fail me.
I have a Father who will never, never fail me.
Jesus is my Father. He will never, never fail me.
Rock of ages, never, never fails.

I DID NOT GIVE UP

We all have our stories to tell about the challenges we face in life. I have many things I could have given up on, but the grace of God kept and protected me from giving up. To Him be the glory, honor and adoration. Amen! The enemy is working so hard to discourage us, mess up our testimonies, steal our joys and blessings in different ways. He will try, but we must keep reminding ourselves that he is a defeated foe, in the mighty name of Jesus. Amen! When we commit everything unto God, allow Him to lead, and we plead His precious blood on EVERYTHING that concerns us, we are applying a very powerful "repellent" that protects us against the plans/attacks of the enemy.

"When it rains, it pours." It has been an amazing journey. Let me share how God kept me from giving up on my nursing career. A professor in one of the nursing schools I attended once told me that I will NEVER be a nurse. The professor did everything in her power, and God allowed her to drop me out of the program for reasons best known to God. I did not understand it then, but it is becoming clearer to me now. I was a licensed practical nurse (LPN) at the time, trying to obtain an associate degree as a registered nurse. God closed the "door" because He had greater plans for me, but I did not understand. I cried and was very devastated because I was looking at the finish line but couldn't finish the race.

When I thought God had opened a better door (a BSN program), I was beaming with joy because it was an accelerated program. I was doing pretty well in the program. Somehow, along the line, I had to withdraw to care for my family. I was to graduate in May with a BSN degree. I left the school in August because of my dedication to my family. Not too long after, I found another school, but unfortunately, my previous nursing classes, including the prerequisites (anatomy and physiology, microbiology and other classes), were not accepted. I had to start all over in the new school, and I had to take the required sciences all over again as well. The disappointments were enough to doubt whether God approved of my nursing career. But the Lord was with me, and He granted me the grace not to give up. I was determined that the negative pronunciation that I will never be a nurse, the obstacles/challenges will build and not break me, in the name of Jesus. Amen!

The mountain seemed insurmountable, but God helped me. Brother/sister, when Jesus says yes, NOBODY can say no. Today, God has helped me become a certified nurse practitioner. I am happy and blessed to be a provider to His glory, honor, and adoration. Hallelujah, Amen! Someone might have prophesied negatively into your life. I pray that God will reverse everything and perfect His will in all that concerns you. May God answer your prayers and grant you all your heart desires, according to His will, in the name of Jesus. To that nursing student who has been dropped out of the program or about to be dropped, that medical student or maybe you are in another profession/career, and you are not sure if you will be able to complete the program. I tell you, if it is ordained by God that you will finish, He will surely see you through, in the name of Jesus. Amen! DO NOT GIVE UP! You can do it with the help of God. It is written: *"Being confident of this very thing, that He who has begun a good work in you will complete it until the day of Jesus Christ"* (Philippians 1:6 NKJV). The Lord has made you head and not tail. I pray that you will soon testify of the goodness of God in your life/career and all areas of your life in the land of the living, in the mighty name of Jesus. Amen. OUR GOD IS ABLE! What the Lord has done for me, I cannot tell it all. I just want to say THANK YOU, LORD, FOR EVERYTHING!

I want to testify of the goodness of God, using my last and first names, my profession and titles (Apata, Bosede. **NURSE** (I was told I would never be a nurse), MSN, FNP-C, PMHNP-BC). These are some of the blessings I received from the Lord in my "wilderness journey." I am using this opportunity to rededicate them unto God, and I pray that they will be used in ways that will bring glory and honor to Him, in the name of Jesus. May God destroy pride; I pray that all the praises and adoration be unto His holy name. May "Adam"/self in me "die" COMPLETELY and may Jesus reign SUPREME in my life and yours, in His holy name. Amen! With my story, I hope you understand why these mean so much to me:

A = Almighty Father, the greatest
P = Physician. The I am that I am.
A = Alpha, Omega, the beginning and the end, has
T = Turned things
A = Around for my good, in the mighty name of Jesus. Amen! I am;

B = Blessed
O = Ordained and
S = Set aside to SHINE for God's glory, in the name of Jesus. Amen!
    I am;
E = Earnestly seeking the face of God and praying to be more
D = Dedicated to His work. I pray for a discerning spirit and
    TOTAL deliverance from the
E = Enemy and his angels/agents, in the name of Jesus. Amen! I am
    absolutely;

N = Nothing without Christ. He is my all in all. His
U = Unlimited grace and favor are upon me. I am;
R = Redeemed and saved by the precious blood of Jesus, shed on
    Calvary. I am;
S = Sanctified, blessed, victorious and marked to be amongst those
    who will spend
E = Eternal life with Jesus, in His mighty and Holy name. Amen!

M = My fellow brothers and sisters, Let's say NO to things that are
    pulling us down. No to;
S = Suicide! No more time for Sin. The wages of sin is death
    (Romans 6:23). Wishing you a
N = New beginning and a new life in Jesus, our Lord and   Savior,
    Amen! You will not

F = Fail, nor be put to shame. Your experience will be from glory to glory

N = New blessings in abundance will be showered upon you and all yours. May the

P = Peace of God that passes human understanding be your portion. May He

C = Complete the good work He has started in you, in the mighty name of Jesus. Amen! I

P = Pray that the

M = Master Savior, faithful Father, Redeemer and Friend, our

H = Healer, Helper, the greatest Physician,

N = Never failing God, will continue to

P = Protect, provide and perfect all that concerns you and your loved ones. May the Lord

B = Bless all your endeavors and lift you up high. I say:

C = COMFORT YE MY PEOPLE! In the mighty name of Jesus, I pray. Amen!

Song of Praise "Na My Testimony" By Henry Nwanguma of the Ambassadors
(written in pidgin English)

Since wey I find Jesus
My life begin dey sweet
Since wey I find Jesus
E-come dey sweet sweet boku.

I no dey tell you fake story-o
E-touch my life oooo
Make you come taste my Lord (X2)

Chorus
E-give me new body
E-give me fresh heart ooo
E-come add many many good thing
Na my testimony o (X2)

Long long time ago, I dey wallow for sin o, I dey waka for the
wrong side.
I no see the good thing wey Jesus keep for me, but today, life
don change for me.
Jesus e-don come give me new body, hey my broda... na my
testimony ooo.

Every day my broda, I dey live happy life, Jesus e-don come
make my heart dey sweet.
Make you come taste my Lord today,
If you call am today e-go answer.
Come give you hope as e-give me, hey my broda...na my
testimony ooo.

Prayer of Dedication

May the Lord keep you in perfect peace, in the name of Jesus (Isaiah 26:3). By the grace of God, as from today, *"You shall go out with joy, and be led out with peace; The mountains and the hills Shall break forth into singing before you, and all the trees of the field shall clap their hands"* (Isaiah 55:12 NKJV), in the name of Jesus. It is written that God will give peace in the land, and you shall lie down, and none will make you afraid; God will rid the land of evil beasts, and the sword will not go through your land, in the mighty name of Jesus (Leviticus 26:6). I decree and declare in that holy and mighty name of Jesus, *"Mercy and truth have met together; Righteousness and peace have kissed"* (Psalm 85:10), in all the areas of your life, in the name of Jesus! *"Now may the God of peace Himself sanctify you completely; and may your whole spirit, soul, and body be preserved blameless at the coming of our Lord Jesus Christ"* (1 Thessalonians 5:23 NKJV). Together, we say goodbye to sorrow, anxiety, depression, or ANYTHING that may affect your joy, peace, and spiritual walk/growth with the Lord, in the mighty name of Jesus, I pray. Amen!

HOW DRY ARE YOUR "BONES?"

S ome challenges in life may seem hopeless and very discouraging. The good news is that we serve a God of impossibilities, and there is NOTHING He cannot do. Hallelujah!

It is written: "*Is anything too hard for the LORD? At the appointed time I will return to you, according to the time of life, and Sarah shall have a son*" (Genesis 18:14 NKJV).

I pray that at God's appointed time, all the closed doors will start to open for you, in the name of Jesus. Humanly speaking, Sarah's "bone" about having a child, was EXTREMELY dry. Hopes were lost. She was doubtful due to her age and her menopausal state. Wouldn't we do the same if we were to be in her shoes? The good news is that: God is FAITHFUL!

Naturally, she accepted defeat, not knowing that God was not done working with her.

"*Then Abraham fell on his face and laughed, and said in his heart, "Shall a child be born to a man who is one hundred years old? And shall Sarah, who is ninety years old, bear a child"* (Genesis 17:17 NKJV).

She didn't take the promise seriously. She laughed. I don't know what you and I would have done.

"Therefore. Sarah laughed within herself, saying, 'After I am waxed old shall I have pleasure, my lord being old also?'" (Genesis 18:12, KJV).

We cannot say that she gave up too soon at her age. She just had to accept what we call the "reality of life," but God proved Himself, showing that NOTHING is over until He says so. May our faith in Him be strengthened, in the name of Jesus. Once there is life, there is hope. The Lord is about to prove Himself in your life. So, don't give up!

Sarah believed that they would have children, but she didn't know they would come through her. She thought she had been restrained by God. So, she tried to help Him out.

It is written: *"Now Sarai, Abram's wife, had borne him no children. And she had an Egyptian maidservant whose name was Hagar. So, Sarai said to Abram, "See now, the LORD has restrained me from bearing children. Please, go in to my maid; perhaps I shall obtain children by her." And Abram heeded the voice of Sarai. Then Sarai, Abram's wife, took Hagar her maid, the Egyptian, and gave her to her husband Abram to be his wife, after Abram had dwelt ten years in the land of Canaan"* (Genesis 16:1-3 NKJV).

Do you feel "restrained" in some areas of your life? Are you about to call on "Hagar" to replace you in the role/s God ordained for you? I pray that NOBODY will take your rightful place, in the name of Jesus. May God give you the grace to hold on tight unto

Him. May He grant you the necessary help needed to persevere to the end, in the mighty name of Jesus. Amen! The world and the people around you may think you are too old for certain blessings. In the sight of God, you will ALWAYS be young. You are a special person, created in God's image, and you mean so much to Him. He can bless you at any time. So, **DO NOT GIVE UP!**

Sometimes, we think we know more than God. We want quick answers to our challenges, and in the process, we get ourselves into unnecessary problems that may result in bringing innocent people into our "mess." Hagar never thought of messing with Abram. Neither did it ever cross Abram's mind to betray or cheat on his wife, despite their condition. The idea came from Sarah.

"So he went in to Hagar, and she conceived. And when she saw that she had conceived, her mistress became despised in her eyes. Then Sarai said to Abram, "My wrong be upon you! I gave my maid into your embrace; and when she saw that she had conceived, I became despised in her eyes. The LORD judge between you and me." So Abram said to Sarai, "Indeed your maid is in your hand; do to her as you please." And when Sarai dealt harshly with her, she fled from her presence" (Genesis 16:4-6).

We are to continue to remind ourselves that GOD DOES NOT NEED OUR HELP! Whatever He promised, He will SURELY deliver. Don't be in a hurry. Do not let your lack of patience bring "Hagar" and "Ishmael" into your "mess." Only God can turn the "mess" into a powerful message, at His own time and in His own way. So, be patient, please.

My beautiful ladies, not every man will be like Abram, oh! Hagar was younger. Her pregnancy seemed like a dream come true. The long-awaited blessings were looking promising through her. My sister, some men will not send "Hagar" away because of you, oh! So, **BE CAREFUL** (laugh with me)! To those of us from Africa, you know even if your husband wants to support you, there may be somebody in his family (or the whole family) who will see to it that you leave your husband's house for "Hagar" to stay, most especially the ones who regard wives as "baby machines." They will start counting the months from the day you become "Mrs." to their family. These people may join "Hagar" in making your life miserable because they would have written you off saying that, for so many years, you have been unable to give them the promised child. It doesn't matter how sweet and amazing you are or have been to them. They may switch gears and go with the one they can benefit from. The truth of life is: "People only know the taste of the food that is in their mouth; once swallowed, they may not remember the taste anymore." Don't let them "swallow" you, please. Just focus on God's promises for you. He is faithful and able to see you through, in the name of Jesus. Amen!

My Darling brother, the Lord is still going to bless you as promised. Be patient and DO NOT GIVE UP! Do not fall for any form of temptation to compromise. Your blessing will not come through any "Hagar." Substitutes are different from the originals.

Do not compound the issues. Wait patiently on God to see you through. So, stay away from the "substitutes," please. The Lord is about to revive the dead wombs; the good Lord will open all the closed doors for you and your wife of many years. Are you willing to forsake what looks like your long-awaited blessings and pleasure of life to be committed and supportive of your wife? Remember, "NOT EVERYTHING THAT GLITTERS IS GOLD." Don't trade what God promised you for something temporary. Only God can make your "dry bone" wet again. Wait for your "promised child."

I want to remind us once again that we serve a God who specializes in making the impossible things possible. He is also a God who keeps His promises.

"And the LORD visited Sarah as He had said, and the LORD did for Sarah as He had spoken. For Sarah conceived and bore Abraham a son in his old age, at the set time of which God had spoken to him. And Abraham called the name of his son who was born to him—whom Sarah bore to him—Isaac"
(Genesis 21:1-3 NKJV).

To those of us in the medical field, we know it was NOTHING but DIVINE INTERVENTION for Sarah and Abraham to have a son. You have waited this long; God has not brought you this far to leave you. He will fulfill what He has promised. He will visit you and surprise you. Your "Isaac" is on the way; divine elevation is coming your way, in the mighty name of Jesus. Amen! Just DON'T GIVE UP!

In what ways do you doubt God today? Let me remind you that God is FAITHFUL and able to see you through. The Lord in His infinite mercies will "IMMERSE" your "dry bones" in His precious blood and make them "wet/juicy" (active/functioning and productive) again. He will cause "breath" to enter into the "dry bones" and bring them back to life, in the mighty name of Jesus. Amen!

"And I will lay sinews upon you, and will bring up flesh upon you, and cover you with skin, and put breath in you, and ye shall live; and ye shall know that I am the LORD. And when I beheld, lo, the sinews and the flesh came up upon them, and the skin covered them above: but there was no breath in them. Then said he unto me, Prophesy unto the wind, prophesy, son of man, and say to the wind, thus saith the Lord GOD; Come from the four winds, O breath, and breathe upon these slain, that they may live. So, I prophesied as he commanded me, and the breath came into them, and they lived, and stood up upon their feet, an exceeding great army" (Ezekiel 37:6, 8, 9 & 10, KJV).

So, prophesy darling child of God to your "dry bones." The God of Ezekiel is also your God. He is alive and ready to breathe His breath of life into any form of "dry bones" you may be dealing with. The Lord will make your roses bloom again; hopes will be restored; doors of blessings/opportunities will be opened, and your tomorrow will be greater than today. Do not give up because you will soon smile/laugh and rejoice in the Lord again, in God's appointed time, in the mighty name of Jesus. Amen!

Song of Meditation "In His Time" By Diane Ball

Prophesy to Your Dry Bones!

It is written: *"Ask, and it will be given to you; seek, and you will find; knock, and it will be opened to you. For everyone who asks receives, and he who seeks finds, and to him who knocks it will be opened. Or what man is there among you who, if his son asks for bread, will give him a stone? Or if he asks for a fish, will he give him a serpent? If you then, being evil, know how to give good gifts to your children, how much more will your Father who is in heaven give good things to those who ask Him"*
(Matthew 7:7-11 NKJV)

Our God is faithful. He has given us the freedom to prophesy in His Holy name, to our "dry bones."

Therefore, prophesy to yourself concerning that sickness: *"I shall not die, but live, and declare the works of the LORD"* (Psalm 118:17). Say to yourself: *"This sickness is not unto death, but for the glory of God, that the Son of God may be glorified through it"* (John 11:4).

Let poverty know that, it is written: "*For the LORD your God will bless you just as He promised you; you shall lend to many nations, but you shall not borrow; you shall reign over many nations, but they shall not reign over you"* (Deuteronomy 15:6).

For that promotion that is long overdue, prophesy: *"And the LORD will make you the head and not the tail; you shall be above only, and not be beneath, if you heed the commandments of the LORD your God, which I command you today, and are careful to observe them"* (Deuteronomy 28:13).

Darling child of God, prophesy. When you are passing through the storms of life, it is written: *When you pass through the waters, I will be with you; and through the rivers, they shall not overflow you. When you walk through the fire, you shall not be burned, nor shall the flame scorch you"* (Isaiah 43:2).

Prophesy as David did, *"Yea, though I walk through the valley of the shadow of death, I will fear no evil; For You are with me; Your rod and Your staff, they comfort me"* (Psalm 23:4).

When you are afraid, prophesy: *"The LORD is my shepherd; I shall not want"* (Psalm 23:1 NKJV).

Tell the "bullies" that it is written: *"The LORD is my light and my salvation; Whom shall I fear? The LORD is the strength of my life; of whom shall I be afraid?"* (Psalm 27:1 NKJV). It is time to tell them: *"The LORD is on my side; I will not fear. What can man do to me?"* (Psalm 118:6 NKJV). Remind yourself of this: *"For God has not given us a spirit of fear, but of power and of love and of a sound mind"* (2 Timothy 1:7 NKJV).

For the intruders in your marriage, trying to break your home, prophesy: "*Wherefore they are no more twain, but one flesh. What therefore God hath joined together, let not man put asunder*" (Matthew 19:6, KJV).

To your children, prophesy: "*And the LORD will make you the head and not the tail; you shall be above only, and not be beneath, if you heed the commandments of the LORD your God, which I command you today, and are careful to observe them*" (Deuteronomy 28:13 NKJV). Prophesy: "*Here am I and the children whom the LORD has given me! We are for signs and wonders in Israel from the LORD of hosts, who dwells in Mount Zion*" (Isaiah 8:18 NKJV). It is written: "*For I will pour water on him who is thirsty and floods on the dry ground; I will pour My Spirit on your descendants, And My blessing on your offspring; They will spring up among the grass like willows by the watercourses.' One will say, 'I am the LORD's'; Another will call himself by the name of Jacob; Another will write with his hand, 'The LORD's,' And name himself by the name of Israel*" (Isaiah 44:3-5 NKJV).

If you are broken-hearted, prophesy: "*My flesh and my heart fail; But God is the strength of my heart and my portion forever*" (Psalm 73:26 NKJV). Hallelujah!

As blurry and as uncertain as things may look, I prophesy that anxiety will not take over your life. Depression will not know your address. I pray that sound mind will be your portion, in the name of Jesus. Amen! Prophesy: *"In the multitude of my anxieties within me, your comforts delight my soul"* (Psalm 94:19 NKJV). Let us agree together with the Lord on the prophesies and seal them with the blood of Jesus. I pray that the peace of God will abide with you today and forever. So, shall it be for you, in the mighty name of Jesus. Amen!

The Lord is with you. He is asking you, (put your name): "Can the "dry bones" live?"

"The hand of the LORD came upon me and brought me out in the Spirit of the LORD, and set me down in the midst of the valley; and it was full of bones. And He said to me, "Son of man, can these bones live?" So, I answered, "O Lord GOD, you know." Again, He said to me, "Prophesy to these bones, and say to them, 'O dry bones, hear the word of the LORD" (Ezekiel 37:1, 3-4)

May God grant all of us the faith to prophesy to our "dry bones," and may they "hear the word of the Lord" and come back to life. Our God is a miracle-working Father. He is able, and He will see us through, in the mighty name of Jesus. Amen!

Song of Meditation "He is Able, Abundantly Able" By Unknown Artiste

HOW DEEP IS YOUR "PIT?"

Y ou may be saying to yourself, "If only Bosede knows how deep the "pit" the enemy has thrown me in is, maybe she would understand my frustration better." You may be saying to yourself, "I don't have a "ladder" to climb out of the "pit' I am in; I have been forsaken. How does she want me to get out of this mess? I have no strength left in me. If only she knew, maybe she would understand that the "pit" is not only deep but also VERY DRY! This is not just a kind of shallow "pit." What part of "I have lost it ALL" does she not understand? I am nobody to everybody. Can you imagine the feeling? All I face is ridicule, shame, just name it. I feel so ashamed of myself, and sometimes, I just wish I could disappear or hide in a cave. Hear me loud and clear, lady B., Just tell me, are we almost home? I **AM TIRED, FRUSTRATED, and I AM HURTING SO BAD. OUCH!**

Bosede, try to empathize, please! I was a little child, innocent and obedient. I was raped by the one I looked up to for protection. I had to live in fear for many years. He saw tears of pain rolling down my cheeks, but he didn't even care. **IT HURTS!**

For your information lady B., she promised to love me. On our wedding day, we both vowed that we would spend the rest of our lives together. She left me for someone else, took off the wedding ring and threw it at me in the presence of our child and walked away as I stood, confused, broken, devastated, hopeless and completely lost. It was very painful to watch her turn her back on me and to accept the "bitter truth" that; I am NOBODY to the one who means the whole world to me. My heart is broken into pieces. I am afraid to love again. Where and how do you want me to start all over again? Bosede, in case you don't know, the type of "wound" I have is deep, "infected," and it has resulted in some form of "amputation" of a very important part of my body. It can NEVER be the same again, with the "prosthesis." Lady B., I was intelligent, talented, full of life, dreams and hope, but EVERYTHING is gone. She left me "naked" and wounded. Ouch, ouch, Bosede; **IT HURTS TO THE BONES!**

I gave her my all and even had a joint account with her, only to find out that I have been betrayed. I was working so hard, but I wasn't paying attention to how the money was being spent. When I asked for money, she would say, "We have used it on something else." I trusted her and did not question ANYTHING. Unfortunately, now that I am becoming so tired and unable to do what I used to do, and I have to deal with the broken heart, she turned her back on me and asked me to go and work for my own money; she showed me the door. She said I should feel free to leave whenever I was ready, in a way that made me feel like a total stranger and unwanted to the love of my life. She even encouraged me to go and die if I want to, that she has moved on.

Unfortunately, the "I" syndrome affected the "we" in us and destroyed EVERYTHING completely. Bosede, **IT HURTS!**

I guess you don't really know how challenging it could be, dealing with some in-laws. Maybe your in-laws are different from mine. Maybe you don't know what it means to deal with difficult people whose goal is to hurt, ridicule and take your meekness for weakness. They come and run my home. I have worked so hard in my life, and they have pushed me away, and they are controlling the affairs in my home because I am regarded as only a baby machine or an acquired property. **IT HURTS!**

How would you handle the shock when you have been told that your spouse should have married another person from your family, that you are not the right one? Unexpectedly, I became "Leah," not "Rachel." **IT HURTS!** How would you feel if you have to suffer in the hands of the ones, you love dearly, where nothing you do is good enough? I tell you, Lady B., **IT HURTS!** I felt so lonely that it seemed that my own shadow was running away from me. You may not understand the pain. Imagine that people only remember you when they need your services, and those same people tell you that you are no fun to be with when you don't have anything to offer. They are experts at playing the victim mentality role, and they project their wrongdoing to make people see you as a bad person. To make matters worse, they tell me all the time that I am the one with issues. So, I started something called "self-evaluation," thinking if more than two or three people are saying the same thing, I must really have issues

24

as they were saying and should do something about it. On the contrary, other people I have encountered see me as a blessing. My environment became so toxic. Lady B., I won't lie to you. I got so confused, lost, lonely and didn't even know what to do. **IT HURTS!**

Do you have any idea of what it means to see your beloved child, who means the whole world to you, heading the wrong way, and you feel so helpless? Bosede, I have done all I could do, but the story is still the same. **IT HURTS!** My story, Lady B., I am that someone who has invested so much in my work, and I was looking forward to retirement, and now, I have been laid off with nothing to show for the investment of many years. **IT HURTS!**

I was in my final year, and I have informed friends and family about my upcoming graduation, only to be dropped out of the program at the last minute because that professor didn't like me. **IT HURTS!**

Bosede, I have degrees like the thermometer. I was brilliant in class. I passed my exams; I am eligible to work, but I have found no job. Those who were to support, encourage and pray with me started calling me names and making fun of me. No matter how hard I tried, I have been unable to secure a job, and the ridicule is so much and unbearable. I tell you, **IT HURTS!**

Okay, my own story, Lady B., is that I left my home country for "greener pasture." I sold EVERYTHING I had, thinking once I get to the new place, I will get a job and will be able to bounce back again. Until now, I have no work papers, so, no job (simple arithmetic)! I left my spouse and children back home with the hope of supporting them financially and later bringing them over. Now, I can't even support myself here, much less support anyone else. I can't go back home and don't even know how or when I will be able to reunite with my family again. I love them dearly, and I miss them so much. You can only imagine the loneliness, guilt and emotional distress. Bosede, **IT HURTS!**

Lady B., I know you are trying to help, but how do I tell my child that their father was sent to jail for a crime he did not commit? Tell me, what words of comfort will heal the "wounds" of someone who lost a dear one who was sentenced to death for a crime he did not commit? How do I explain to my child that he may be persecuted because of his color? It is not fair, and **IT HURTS!** Listen, Bosede, how do you comfort someone whose family died a painful death for no reason? He was pleading for breath, but the one kneeling on his neck would not get off and watched him die the painful death, as he was calling on his mother, while others watched with no compassion or any sense of remorse. How do I explain that type of cruelty to his children? How can anyone understand this deep pain, Lady B.? **IT HURTS TO THE BONES!**

Listen, he was just jugging to maintain good health. We had plans. I was expecting him back home, but my expectation of his return was shattered because someone just decided to kill him. He didn't do anything, only to find out that His God-given color was the

26

reason someone hated him so much and killed him. Imagine that Bosede, **IT HURTS!**

We were in our motherland, enjoying the company of families and friends when they came. They captured us as slaves, separated husbands from wives, children from parents; they molested, raped and did all the havoc they could do to us. They took us away from the motherland and brought us to a strange land. They used us. Now, they are doing everything to get rid of us. Some of us don't even know the way back home. The only place we know as home here on earth is here, but we are not wanted. We don't feel safe. Ouch! Bosede, **IT HURTS!**

Our threshold for pain is different, so are the types of pain we bear. For me, Lady B., I get anxious every month when I do the pregnancy test. This has been going on for years now. The story is still the same. **IT HURTS!** Listen Bosede, after many years of waiting, I became pregnant, and everyone was happy. We had names we wanted to give the baby; the nursery room was decorated. We bought clothes, had a baby shower; friends came with gifts and rejoiced with us. We were happy and longing for the arrival of our "bundle of joy." I carried the pregnancy to full term, experienced the excruciating pain of labor, but complications started, and I had to go through an emergency cesarean section. Despite all of this, it was a stillbirth. **IT HURTS!**

Lady B., kindly give me the chance to express my own story, please. I dropped off my ONLY precious child at school, and he got shot with other innocent children and some of the teachers. **IT HURTS!** Waking up in the morning only to see a family member you love dearly dead due to suicide, the memory is fresh. I kept asking myself, "Where did I drop the ball? What could I have done better?" Bosede, **IT HURTS!**

There are others with different kinds of hurts that are unspoken. Many souls are hurting and dying. I'm praying for healing, in the mighty name of Jesus. Amen!

Darling brother/sister in the Lord, believe me, I hear you, and I can only imagine your pain. I sympathize with you and pray that God will heal your wounds, in the name of Jesus. It may appear like there is no way out now. Others may underestimate the level of pain you are bearing, and I may not be able to fix your broken heart or soothe your pain the way you want, but I know a Man who can! His name is Jesus. He is our Savior, Redeemer and our dear Friend. He is able to heal your wounds and restore your joy in His holy name. Amen! I am pleading that you give Him a chance to help you. The challenges have tortured you enough. It is time to introduce your MIGHTY GOD to those "big" problems. The God of Joseph, who brought him out of the pit, is alive, He is your God too, and He is able to bring you out if you don't give up and you surrender ALL to Him.

God wants you to be patient. Let Him display his PROFESSIONALISM of making the impossible things possible.

"Every valley shall be exalted and every mountain and hill brought low; The crooked places shall be made straight and the rough places smooth" (Isaiah 40:4).

The Lord is saying to you today, *"Come to Me, all you who labor and are heavy laden, and I will give you rest"* (Matthew 11:28).

The Lord will comfort you. He will give you rest; He will bring you out of the "pit" of pain and sorrow. To answer your question: "Are we almost home?" I say YES! Jesus is coming very soon. The long, "dark night" is almost gone (HALLELUJAH)! Be courageous. The "battle" is almost over. Until then, may the good Lord heal your broken heart and grant you the grace to smile, laugh and be the happy you again, in the mighty name of Jesus. Amen! **DO NOT GIVE UP, PLEASE!**

Song of Meditation "I Know A Man Who Can" By George Jones/Barry Smith

Song of Meditation "How Far from Home?" By Annie Rebekah Smith (1853)

How far from home? I asked, as on

I bent my steps—the watchman spake:

"The long, dark night is almost gone,

The morning soon will break.

29

Then weep no more, but speed thy flight,
With Hope's bright star thy guiding ray,
Till thou shalt reach the realms of light,
In everlasting day."

I asked the warrior on the field;
This was his soul-inspiring song:
"With courage bold, the sword I'll wield,
The battle is not long.
Then weep no more, but well endure
The conflict, till thy work is done;
For this we know, the prize is sure,
When victory is won."

I asked again; earth, sea, and sun
Seemed, with one voice, to make reply:
"Time's wasting sands are nearly run,
Eternity is nigh.
Then weep no more—with warning tones,
Portentous sights are thick'ning round,
The whole creation, waiting, groans,
To hear the trumpet sound."

Not far from home! O blessed thought!
The trav'ler's lonely heart to cheer;
Which oft a healing balm has brought,
And dried the mourner's tear.
Then weep no more, since we shall meet

Where weary footsteps never roam—
Our trials past, our joys complete,
Safe in our Father's home.

YOU ARE THE CHOSEN ONE!

With God on your side, you are more than the majority and more than a conqueror. No matter your past, pain or status, with God on your side, NO ONE can take your rightful place. People may have more qualifications than you do for that vacant position. It is possible that you didn't even see yourself as someone qualified either. So, you didn't even bother to apply. If God says that the position is yours, by His grace, your destiny helper will come looking for you. Just be faithful in whatever position or situation you find yourself now. I pray, in the name of Jesus; God's mercy, favor, blessings and ALL the good things of life will follow you. Just be patient. Continue to trust and obey God. You have been chosen by Him, and your destiny helper is on the way to "anoint" you and give you an AMAZING position that is beyond your imagination, in the mighty name of Jesus. Amen!

Remember David's story:

"Now the LORD said to Samuel, "How long will you mourn for Saul, seeing I have rejected him from reigning over Israel? Fill your horn with oil, and go; I am sending you to Jesse the Bethlehemite. For I have provided Myself a king among his sons." And Samuel said, "How can I go? If Saul hears it, he will kill me." But the LORD said, "Take a heifer with you, and say, 'I have come to sacrifice to the LORD.' Then invite Jesse to the sacrifice, and I

will show you what you shall do; you shall anoint for Me the one I name to you" (1 Samuel 16:1-3 NKJV). Your name is about to be announced for promotion, honor and God's blessings, in the mighty name of Jesus. Amen!

Maybe your family was invited to a "party" but you have been excluded. Sorry! They may not be aware of the greatness in you YET! They may have taken you for granted and thought your present situation dictates your greatness. I am telling you that God is about to prove them wrong. Don't compete with anyone; be gentle, loving, respectful, caring and make it a point of duty to help others as much as you can. Darling brother/sister in the Lord, get yourself a "comfortable chair," stop stressing and watch God turn things around in your favor, in the name of Jesus. Amen! Your family may not be proud of you YET, but God is, and He is all that should matter. You will soon be honored in the precious name of Jesus. Amen!

We are in a world where money, position, looks or earthly possessions dictate how people treat you. People are grouped into different classes (high, middle or low). Let me tell you: No class is higher than being a child of the Most High God. Hallelujah, Amen! So, keep your head up. Before long, they will come looking for you.

"Men look at the outward appearance, but God looks at the heart" (1 Samuel 16:7).

Don't let people's opinion of you disturb or surprise you. People make the mistake of judging other people by their outward appearances. The prophet Samuel made the same mistake. When he saw Eliab, he said, "Surely the LORD's anointed is before Him!" Little did he know that the chosen one was still with the sheep. Continue with what you are doing and wait patiently for God to bring you out for good.

"So, Samuel did what the LORD said, and went to Bethlehem. And the elders of the town trembled at his coming, and said, "Do you come peaceably?" And he said, "Peaceably; I have come to sacrifice to the LORD. Sanctify yourselves, and come with me to the sacrifice." Then he consecrated Jesse and his sons, and invited them to the sacrifice. So it was, when they came, that he looked at Eliab and said, "Surely the LORD's anointed is before Him!" But the LORD said to Samuel, "Do not look at his appearance or at his physical stature, because I have refused him. For the LORD does not see as man sees; for man looks at the outward appearance, but the LORD looks at the heart." So, Jesse called Abinadab, and made him pass before Samuel. And he said, "Neither has the LORD chosen this one." Then Jesse made Shammah pass by. And he said, "Neither has the LORD chosen this one." Thus, Jesse made seven of his sons pass before Samuel. And Samuel said to Jesse, "The LORD has not chosen these." And Samuel said to Jesse, "Are all the young men here?" Then he said, "There remains yet the youngest, and there he is, keeping the sheep." And Samuel said to Jesse, "Send and bring him. For we

will not sit down till he comes here." So, he sent and brought him in. Now he was ruddy, with bright eyes, and good-looking. And the LORD said, "Arise, anoint him; for this is the one!" Then Samuel took the horn of oil and anointed him in the midst of his brothers; and the Spirit of the LORD came upon David from that day forward. So, Samuel arose and went to Ramah"
(1 Samuel 16:4-13 NKJV).

Your dream of greatness will not be aborted, and no one will take your rightful place, in the mighty name of Jesus. Amen! DO NOT GIVE UP, PLEASE!

Your family might have left you out, even though your whole family was invited. They may see you as someone who does not belong to the "class" of those worthy of attending the party. Darling brother/sister in the Lord, don't you know that you are blessed, and nobody can curse you?

"Behold, I have received a command to bless; He has blessed, and I cannot reverse it" (Numbers 23:20 NKJV).

Yes, indeed, you are blessed, and no one can reverse it. The enemy will try, but He has failed. The ones blessing you will be blessed, and those cursing you are cursed, in the name of Jesus. The "party" cannot start until you are located and brought there.

The Lord will make you so important that NOBODY will be able to sit until you arrive at the scene. You will be too important to be ignored. "Who is she/he?" will now become "Where is she/he?" in the mighty name of Jesus. Amen! You are about to be

35

ANOINTED, and your story will NEVER be the same. The spirit of God will rest upon you and ALL yours, in the mighty name of Jesus. Amen!

Song of Meditation "Anointing, Fall on Me" By Unknown Artiste

Anointing, fall on me.

Anointing, fall on me.

May the power of the Holy Ghost fall on me.

Anointing fall on me.

Maybe things are taking longer than expected, and now you feel so tired and overwhelmed. You may be at the stage where the pain seems so unbearable, and you are contemplating killing yourself. I am pleading with you to hold on a little longer, please. "This too shall pass," God's anointing is about to fall on you, in the name of Jesus. Amen! The storm is almost over. Your breakthrough is closer than you can ever imagine. The blessings—the job, children, loving and caring spouse—are in the making. The "prodigal" child, spouse, parents are on their way to "Damascus," where the Holy Spirit will "arrest" them, and they will NEVER be the same. Your "soul" will soon be converted to "Paul," in the name of Jesus. God's elected "Ananias" is already on his way to "Straight Street," where God will prepare them for His glory (Acts 9:1-22). Their names will be changed, and they will NEVER be the same again, in the mighty name of Jesus. Amen!

Just be patient. Allow God to hold you close to Him. Do not let depression, anxiety, disappointments and the cares of this world get you down. The Lord is with you. He loves you.

"Yet now be strong, Zerubbabel,' says the LORD; 'and be strong, Joshua, son of Jehozadak, the high priest; and be strong, all you people of the land,' says the LORD, 'and work; for I am with you,' says the LORD of hosts. 'According to the word that I covenanted with you when you came out of Egypt, so My Spirit remains among you; do not fear" (Haggai 2:4-5 NKJV).

Song of Meditation "Fear Not" By Banji Fadehan

Fear not, be not afraid.

Fear not, be not afraid.

My Grace is all enough for you,

Be not Afraid.

Personalize the above scripture. Put your name where those other names are and claim the promises. Be strong. The Lord is with you, and His spirit will never depart from you, in the mighty name of Jesus. Amen! May your focus be on Jesus Christ, who loves you dearly. It is written: *"Let your eyes look straight ahead, and your eyelids look right before you. Ponder the path of your feet and let all your ways be established. Do not turn to the right or the left; Remove your foot from evil"* (Proverbs 4:25-27 NKJV). The Lord will guide and keep you, in the mighty name of Jesus. Amen! DO NOT GIVE UP, PLEASE!

Song of Meditation "I Almost Let Go" By Kurt Carr

POWER OF FORGIVENESS

S ome people might have contributed to your pains and aches. They might have forgotten all they did to you and have moved on. You are unable to progress, unable to sleep well, and things seem to be stagnant. It is time to plead for grace and God's help to be able to forgive—not for the sake of the ones who have hurt you but for your own sanity, sound health and relationship with God. Exhale the old air and inhale the new. I pray that God will purify your heart, in the mighty name of Jesus. Amen!

Unforgiveness can steal your joy. It could affect your health adversely, and you may have to pay for it in ways that may affect you negatively. The truth is, forgiving those who have hurt us can be a very "bitter pill" to swallow, sometimes. Notwithstanding, God has instructed us to forgive, and He will work with us if we give him a chance. May He marinate the "bitter pill" with "honey" and make it palatable and easy to swallow, in the name of Jesus. Amen!

"But if you do not forgive men their trespasses, neither will your Father forgive your trespasses" (Matthew 6:15 NKJV).

"If I regard iniquity in my heart, the Lord will not hear" (Psalm 66:18 NKJV).

When we forgive, our minds will be light and free of UNNECESSARY burden. Not only that, but we will also enjoy the forgiveness of God and others we might have offended as well. We are all sinners in need of God's forgiveness. It is written: *"Blessed are the pure in heart, for they shall see God"* (Matthew 5:8 NKJV). May God help us all, in the name of Jesus. Amen!

Furthermore, may God help us to guard our hearts and minds against the attacks of the enemy. When our minds/hearts are disturbed and clogged up with unforgiveness, it often leads to bitterness, thus inviting depression, anxiety and other medical, social and physical issues. The Bible says, *"Keep your heart with all diligence, for out of it spring the issues of life"* (Proverbs 4:23). We cannot do any of these by ourselves. We need God's help and guidance. Therefore, I pray that God will create in us clean hearts and renew steadfast spirits within us (Psalm 51:10). May God help us all, in the name of Jesus. Amen!

Consider all that Joseph's brothers did to him. He had the right to be very bitter and take revenge, but he chose to forgive instead. When you do good to those who have hurt you, they may be afraid and confused because they don't really know what you are up to, most especially when they know how they would have dealt with you if the tables were to be turned. Darling brother/sister, God is love. May we be like Him, in the name of Jesus. Amen! Joseph's brothers were afraid. So, they pleaded for forgiveness. Because of

Joseph's forgiving spirit, everything turned out to be a very happy reunion with some forms of emotional moments attached to it. God knows that you are the one with the forgiving spirit He can rely on to save your family. He knows you are generous, and you will bless everyone around you, even those who have betrayed and hurt you badly. God is counting on you to bless His children with the blessings He is about to shower on you.

"When Joseph's brothers saw that their father was dead, they said, "Perhaps Joseph will hate us, and may actually repay us for all the evil which we did to him." So, they sent messengers to Joseph, saying, "Before your father died, he commanded, saying, 'Thus you shall say to Joseph: "I beg you, please forgive the trespass of your brothers and their sin; for they did evil to you." 'Now, please, forgive the trespass of the servants of the God of your father." And Joseph wept when they spoke to him. Then his brothers also went and fell down before his face, and they said, "Behold, we are your servants" (Genesis 50:15-18 NKJV).

Joseph was able to forgive His brothers, realizing that God turned their evil intentions to good. May the almighty God turn the evil plans of your enemy around for good and make you victorious, in the name of Jesus. *"Joseph said to them, "Do not be afraid, for am I in the place of God? But as for you, you meant evil against me; but God meant it for good, in order to bring it about as it is this day, to save many people alive. Now therefore, do not be afraid; I will provide for you and your little ones." And he*

40

comforted them and spoke kindly to them" (Genesis 50:19-21 NKJV).

We are human, and we have feelings. We may be able to forgive, but to forget the wrongdoing may not be that easy. Notwithstanding, may we not be bitter; may we be able to remember that God knows why He allows things to happen to us. May His holy name be praised in our lives, no matter the trials, in the mighty name of Jesus. Amen!

Let me quickly inform you that some people do not want to be forgiven, no matter how hard you try. They just want to keep on hurting you; they enjoy seeing you hurt. The interesting thing is that God still wants you to forgive them anyway, but you have to learn to love them from afar because of how toxic associating with them could be.

There is a Yoruba adage that says, "If you have to eat with the 'devil,' your spoon has to be very long." May God guide and teach us how to survive with the "wolves" all around, in the name of Jesus. Amen! Maybe you are confused and wondering how many times one has to forgive. You are not alone. Peter wondered too.

"Then Peter came to Him and said, "Lord, how often shall my brother sin against me, and I forgive him? Up to seven times?" Jesus said to him, "I do not say to you, up to seven times, but up to seventy times seven" (Matthew 18:21-22 NKJV).

Interesting, isn't it? As sinners, we were condemned to die, but we serve a loving, caring and forgiving God, who came to die, for us to be saved. He paid it ALL on the cross of Calvary. Jesus paid all that we could NEVER pay. That is the reason you and I can sing a brand-new song. Hallelujah! May God help us all to be forgiving and be like Him, in the mighty name of Jesus.

"But God demonstrates His own love toward us, in that while we were still sinners, Christ died for us" (Romans 5:8 NKJV).

Song of Meditation "He paid The Debt He Did Not Owe" By Unknown Artiste

He paid the debt he did not owe.

I owe the debt I could not pay.

I needed someone to wash away my sins.

And now I sing a brand-new song.

Amazing Grace

How Jesus paid all that I could never pay

SHOW YOUR REAL FACE

The truth is that we all have issues. It is just that some of us know how to cover things up more than others. Now, let us talk a little about **BEING REAL**. The analogy I want to use is about my "makeup" (cosmetic) experience. I am a lady who does not know how to wear heavy makeup. All I do is put on very light powder, but I see to it that my eyebrows are shaped correctly. Because of my eyebrows, I was given a nickname when I was in Nigeria, "ojú tó n sòrò" (the eyes that talk). I pray that the words my eyes and my whole life will convey will be words of hope, comfort and healing to all. May they be words that will bring souls to the Lord, in the name of Jesus. Amen! I am grateful to those who appreciate this ARTISTIC work of God in me (laugh with me). May the glory of God continue to shine in and through all of us, in the name of Jesus. Amen!

Before going to my story, there is a little exercise we might enjoy when we look in the mirror in the morning. It may help nourish our souls and boast our self-esteem/confidence. The exercise is simple: We look in the mirror and tell ourselves, "Good morning, beautiful/handsome! God is in TOTAL CONTROL of ALL your affairs today and ALWAYS. He does not need your help. Relax and enjoy your beautiful day, SUNSHINE!" Then, blow yourself a big kiss and declare the promises of God, *"I am fearfully and wonderfully made"* (Psalm 139:14).

Love and appreciate what you see in the mirror. It will help you to appreciate God, and you will also love yourself more. If you do not love or appreciate yourself, others might not. It takes a real child of God to commend you and bring out the best in you for others to see and appreciate. Criticism seems to be easier and cheaper than praise from others.

So, make it a point of duty to celebrate yourself. Look in the mirror and tell yourself: I am beautiful, intelligent and lovable. Tell yourself all that you want to hear from people, and you may not feel too bad if you do not hear it from them. When you do, you remind yourself of how God sees you, not just to make yourself happy. Remember that those who mind how you look, those who have problems with your status/condition or have issues with you, will not see the good in you and will try to paint you bad. Therefore, comments from these people should not be taken to heart, to the point that, even when they tell you that you look beautiful, say thank you but kindly check your mirror to see that there is no crust in your eyes or boogers in your nose, to prevent unnecessary embarrassment/ridicule. Lord have mercy!

Those who genuinely love you will ALWAYS look out for your good. They see and accept you just the way God created you.

"The LORD has appeared of old to me, saying: "Yes, I have loved you with an everlasting love; Therefore, with lovingkindness I have drawn you" (Jeremiah 31:3 NKJV).

Darling child of God, YOU ARE BEAUTIFUL/HANDSOME and a VERY IMPORTANT PERSON (VIP), to God Almighty!

Back to my "makeup" experience. During our first daughter's wedding, the children insisted that I wear makeup and artificial eyelashes. I wanted to make my daughter and the rest of the children happy more so that it is not contrary to my faith. So, I did not object to their suggestions. Guess what? It was a remarkably interesting and amazing experience. I really enjoyed my session with the makeup artist. I don't think she had ever taken care of a client as challenging as I was. Can you imagine that someone who does not know how to apply or wear makeup would question EVERYTHING the makeup artist was doing? But she was very patient, and she took the time to explain everything to me, step by step, even though I was slowing her down.

At one point, when I saw that my face was "plastered" with different colors of powder and other things, I was baffled and asked her to stop because I did not like the way I looked. Everyone in the room was laughing because of my "drama." The makeup artist saw that she was not getting anywhere with me. So, she called my daughter, who persuaded me to let the lady finish what she was doing before saying anything. The lady and my daughter

45

knew what the outcome would look like, but I did not. I was not cooperating with them and was too much in a hurry to see the end result. They took the mirror away from me so that I would not see what the makeup artist was doing until she finished.

Sincerely, that was what they should have done from the beginning because we were able to save a lot of time this way. I did not see what she was doing, but I believed my daughter that I would be happy with the result. When I finally surrendered to the makeup artist's professionalism, the transformation was so amazing that I did not even recognize myself when they gave the mirror back to me (very interesting and funny at the same time).

The take-home point here is: Beautiful things that are in the making may initially look very "nasty." With patience, trust in the Lord, endurance and TOTAL surrender to the one in charge (God), the end result is always glorious! The Lord may need to take the "mirror" away from us sometimes to prevent ANYTHING that may stand in His way of Him perfecting His will in our lives.

In my case, after everything was done, my husband's face brightened when he saw me. My father, father-in-law, siblings, other family members and friends could not recognize me. I felt so good, and my head was up high in TOTAL adoration to God. I had this big smile that even added to the beauty, to the glory of God. It was an AMAZING and a beautiful experience I will never forget!

As I recount this experience, I would like to say: Thank you, my beautiful, loving and caring children. Your own children will beautify and take very good care of you too, in the name of Jesus. I love you all. Thanks to the makeup artist as well. Remain blessed.

May we surrender EVERYTHING to God, our Potter, acknowledging that we are the clay. May we let go of the "mirror" and allow Him to mold us after His will, trusting that He will do His best in our lives, in the mighty name of Jesus. Amen!

Song of Meditation "Have Thine Own Way, Lord!" By Adelaide A. Pollard (1906)

1. Have thine own way lord!

Have thine own way!

Thou art the porter,

I am the clay.

Mold me and make me,

After thy will,

While I am waiting, yielded and still.

2. Have thine own way lord!

Have thine own way!

Search me and try me,

Master today!

Whiter than snow Lord,

Wash me just now,

As in thy presence humbly I bow.

3. Have thine own way lord!

Have thine own way!

O for my being absolute sway,

Filled with thy Spirit.

Till all can see, Christ only always living in me.

BEST CONCEALER EVER

Thank God for the different kinds of powders ladies wear, especially the ones called concealers. I tell you, no one should underestimate the awesome, "magical" power of CONCEALERS! According to their names, they conceal spots or skin blemishes. The outcome/effect of makeup can be very interesting, amazing and very deceptive. I heard a joke about a man who decided to sue his wife for "fraud" because he did not know she had tribal marks on her face throughout their dating period. Alas, he saw them after the concealers were wiped off her face. Don't get me wrong, please. There is nothing wrong with tribal marks. The point here is openness. The story was told that the lady covered her tribal marks up from the man until they were married and he felt deceived. My mother had tribal marks, and she was exceptionally BEAUTIFUL! May her gentle soul continue to rest in peace. My father, aunties, some cousins and friends have tribal marks, and they are adorable. We are Africans. Once you see the marks, you will be able to know the tribe one is from. If you are interested in knowing more about tribal marks and the significance, consult with me later (laugh with me)!

For the single men planning to get married, don't say I didn't tell you. If all you see in the one you are planning to marry is a "painted face," I think it is time for an early-morning surprise visit (laugh with me). For men covering up under "Just for Men" (hair color), toupee (for the bald part) or other things, let us be honest. Bear in mind that love covers EVERYTHING and that; "beauty is in the eye of the beholder." That thing we are trying to cover up may be something that will fascinate that special someone who will love and appreciate us, naturally. It is absolutely important that the foundation of our love/relationships is not based on any form of lies (this goes both ways for males and females).

Believe me, ANYTHING based on deception will not last. More importantly, anyone who will not accept or love you the way you are is not worthy of your love. Do your makeup and things to beautify you for fun and not for concealing or distorting the truth. REMEMBER! We are created in God's image. So, naturally, we are beautiful.

"So God created man in His own image; in the image of God, He created him; male and female He created them"
(Genesis 1:27 NKJV).

Do not forget that God took special time to create you. It is written: *"I will praise You, for I am **fearfully** and **wonderfully** made; Marvelous are Your works, and that my soul knows very well"* (Psalm 139:14 NKJV; emphasis added). Darling child of God, you are BEAUTIFUL/HANDSOME, with or without the "additions." May the glory of God continue to shine in and through you, in the mighty name of Jesus. Amen!

Our divine "makeover artist," Jesus, has used His precious blood, shed on the cross of Calvary as a CONCEALER—the type that does not only cover our "blemishes" but REMOVES them PERMANENTLY! Our sins, shame, pain, illnesses, anxiety, depression (or whatever it may be that is not making us live a fulfilled life) are canceled and REMOVED with the blood of Jesus. Amen! It is written, *"Being justified freely by His grace through the redemption that is in Christ Jesus, whom God set forth as a propitiation by His blood, through faith, to demonstrate His righteousness, because in His forbearance God had passed over the sins that were previously committed"* (Romans 3:24-25 NKJV). We are covered with the blood of Jesus. We are not only beautiful, but we are strengthened and untouchable. It is written: *"For the life of the flesh is in the blood, and I have given it to you upon the altar to make atonement for your souls; for it is the blood that makes atonement for the soul"* (Leviticus 17:11 NKJV). I pray that the blood of Jesus will NEVER lose its power, in our lives, in His holy name, I pray. Amen!

Song of Meditation "Nothing but The Blood of Jesus" By Robert Lowry (1876)

1. What can wash away my sin?

Nothing but the blood of Jesus.

What can make me whole again?

Nothing but the blood of Jesus.

Refrain

O precious is the flow

that makes me white as snow;

51

no other fount I know;

nothing but the blood of Jesus.

2. For my pardon this I see:

nothing but the blood of Jesus.

For my cleansing, this my plea:

nothing but the blood of Jesus.

3. Nothing can for sin atone:

nothing but the blood of Jesus.

Naught of good that I have done:

nothing but the blood of Jesus.

4. This is all my hope and peace:

nothing but the blood of Jesus.

This is all my righteousness:

nothing but the blood of Jesus.

Prayer

Thank you, heavenly Father, we plead that you please take off the makeup/veil on our faces and replace them with your glory, Lord! Remind us that You did not promise ONLY sunshine. You said in your word: *"These things I have spoken to you, that in me you may have peace. In the world you will have tribulation; but be of good cheer, I have overcome the world"* (John 16:33 NKJV). Remind us, Father, that we are overcomers through

Christ and His precious blood on the cross of Calvary. Hallelujah! Help us have the courage to accept and appreciate the AMAZING job and the time you invested in creating us. Help us stop pretending to be who or what we are not. May your glory continue to shine in our lives, in the mighty name of Jesus. Amen!

ARE YOU READY FOR JESUS' TRANSFORMATION?

Even though God knows everything, He will NEVER force Himself on us. One Yoruba adage says, "A child that wants to be carried must have his/her arms widely opened." Jesus is at the door knocking, patiently waiting and ready to come in, only if we open the door for Him. He will not break the door or force His way through. Jesus is the greatest "makeover artist" who can transform you and me in the twinkle of an eye if we let Him. He does not need any powder; His blood is the best concealer that can remove our sins/blemishes. The blood of Jesus serves as a "magic eraser." Hallelujah! The "makeover" Jesus gives us is free and does not wash off, no matter the amount of "sweat," "sunshine" or "rain." As long as we remain under His wings/umbrella, we can be assured of His protection. The transformation is unexplainable. If we surrender TOTALLY to Him, our lives will never be the same. What can wash our sins/blemishes away? NOTHING but the blood of Jesus. May we be "washed" clean, in His mighty and holy name. Amen!

As wonderful as one may look with the makeup the world gives, once it is washed off, everything returns to square one (the original look) until it is done all over again. With our God, we remain beautiful and gorgeous if we are constantly connected to Him and "washed" in the precious blood of the lamb. The more time we spend in His presence, the more radiant we become.

54

Amen! A good example is the shining Face of Moses after he came down from Mount Sinai.

"When Moses came down from Mount Sinai with the two tablets of the covenant law in his hands, he was not aware that his face was radiant because he had spoken with the LORD. When Aaron and all the Israelites saw Moses, his face was radiant, and they were afraid to come near him" (Exodus 34:29-30NIV). I pray that the glory of God will shine so bright in you to the point that the enemy will be afraid to come near you and your household, in the mighty name of Jesus. Amen!

Song of Meditation: "Have You Been to Jesus For the Cleansing Power?" E. A. Hoffman (1878)

1. Have you been to Jesus for the cleansing power?
Are you washed in the blood of the Lamb?
Are you fully trusting in His grace this hour?
Are you washed in the blood of the Lamb?

Chorus:
Are you washed in the blood,
In the soul cleansing blood of the Lamb?
Are your garments spotless?
Are they white as snow?
Are you washed in the blood of the Lamb?

2. Are you walking daily by the Savior's side?
Are you washed in the blood of the Lamb?

Do you rest each moment in the Crucified?

Are you washed in the blood of the Lamb?

3. When the Bridegroom cometh will your robes be white?

Are you washed in the blood of the Lamb?

Will your soul be ready for the mansions bright,

And be washed in the blood of the Lamb?

4. Lay aside the garments that are stained with sin,

And be washed in the blood of the Lamb;

There's a fountain flowing for the soul unclean,

O be washed in the blood of the Lamb!

YOU CANNOT FOOL GOD

Isn't it funny the way we are vastly different individuals when we are in our homes/secret corners compared to when we are in public (church, office, school or other social places)? We try to put up our best and cover up our "wounds." We deceive ourselves and the people around us. We sometimes try to fool God, forgetting that we cannot play hide and seek with Him. He knows EVERYTHING about us. The Seventh Day Adventists have a popular way of greeting on Sabbath: "Happy Sabbath." Believe me, not every Sabbath is a happy one for everyone. Many times, some of us just know how to wear the "makeup" or "veil" to cover many things up.

You might be surprised that the church pastor might have just finished crying in his/her office before mounting the pulpit to preach. He/she might still say "Happy Sabbath" to his/her congregation. I don't know how other worshipers greet themselves, but we all have our ways of covering things up: "It is well," "I am blessed," "God is good," and many more. I am the chief of sinners when it comes to this. "It is well," is my favorite one. I call it "positive confession" or "positive declaration," trusting God that things will change for good. I have realized that there is time for everything—time to be real and time to apply "positive confession." Due to the bad experiences, I had talking to people, I decided to keep to myself just to prevent unnecessary

57

ridicule, shame or embarrassment. Instead of talking to people or bottling things up, I journal, then burn or rip it off after I am done. Sometimes, I keep them. I am grateful to God because He helped me turn my pain into prayer/praises. I have six worship albums now. He has given me the ability to encourage others on social media, and He blessed me with the inspiration to write this book. All of these, to the glory of God. May His Holy name be FOREVER PRAISED. Amen!

Even if you succeed at fooling others, you cannot fool them forever. Soon, the truth will be discovered. For instance, I got into trouble one day trying to "cover up." It was one of those challenging days with a lot on my mind. I managed to wear my "readymade" smile and was in "it is well" mode. As I was going along, a sister saw me and decided to talk to me. As we were talking, this "sister" in the Lord didn't know that it was just my body that she was seeing—my mind was somewhere else. In my mind, I was rushing to finish up with the shopping, get food ready for my family before they come back from school/work and complete an assignment that was due that day (I was in school at the time).

As she talked, I was smiling, nodding my head, behaving as if I was with her. She did not understand what was going on until she told me that she lost a family member, and I said, "Oh, that is nice." Lord have mercy! My response was so off, and I didn't even know what was going on. Instead of getting mad at me, she held me close and said, "Bosede, this is NOT you! I just told you

58

someone died, and you said, 'that was nice.'" Just imagine yourself in my shoes at that time. How would you feel? She reported that she has done something like that before. She said, "I know you didn't hear me." I felt so bad, but I was grateful that she could relate to my absentmindedness at that time. I was embarrassed. I apologized and expressed my condolences in tears. We cried and prayed together. After the prayer, she said, "This is the you I know." The take-home message: There is no "super" woman/man. The ones trying to act that way have died. We must be real. When we are tired, we are tired. We must stop pretending to be who we are not. I pray that God will help us be real with Him, in the mighty name of Jesus. Amen! The truth is: WE ALL HAVE ISSUES, and EVERYONE NEEDS SOMEONE. Most importantly, WE ALL NEED JESUS!

Sometimes, I wonder if Christianity is make-believe or a pretense game. I tell you: NO, IT IS NOT! We Christians are the greatest pretenders I have ever known, and I am also very guilty, as you might have read earlier. We try to "cover up" for Jesus. He did not ask us to do this for Him. By now, some of us must have known that it is a very "wonderful" (challenging) experience to be a Christian. If we have carefully read the invitation card Jesus gave us when He was calling us to follow Him, it could have helped us better understand what we signed up for. There would have been no need to want to cover up or think that Christians are not supposed to have challenges. There is no mistake in whatever God does. He directs the wind anyhow and anywhere He wants. This is why we call Him KÁBÍÈSÌ, in the Yoruba language (Who can question you, Lord?).

This is the invitation letter to the followers of Christ. It is written, *"Then Jesus said to His disciples, "If anyone desires to come after Me, let him deny himself, and **TAKE UP HIS CROSS, AND FOLLOW ME"*** (Matthew 16:24 NKJV; emphasis added). The cross could be very heavy if we try to carry it by ourselves. Do not try it, please. When we try to wear the "veil/makeup" and pretend to be who or what we are not, believe me, the "cross" could be UNNECESSARILY and EXTREMELY heavy for us to bear. If we are open and let God be God, He will see us through. It is written: *"Cast your burden on the LORD, and He shall sustain you; He shall never permit the righteous to be moved"* (Psalm 55:22 NKJV). This is the message of God to you today: *"Fear not, for I am with you; Be not dismayed, for I am your God. I will strengthen you, yes, I will help you, I will uphold you with my righteous right hand"* (Isaiah 41:10 NKJV).

As Christians, we think we are to live a life of perfection or pretense to be the "true Christians" we profess to be. Most of us are bleeding/dying inside but still going about with our beautiful, well-fitted "veil/makeup" because we want to make Jesus "look good." May God forgive us! We must remind ourselves that God is good, ALL the time! Nothing we do or don't do can make Him look good or bad. ALL the time, our God is good! He is an awesome God. So, take off the "veil" and bring your burdens to Him. We have the privilege to carry EVERYTHING to God in prayer. Stop carrying the UNNECESSARY garbage by yourself. Your heart may be so heavy, lonely and dreary and your days filled with all sorts of challenges. What a friend we have in our Lord Jesus, Savior and Redeemer! He is our burden bearer. He is very near and ready to take the burdens away from us, in His Holy name. Amen!

Song of Meditation "What A Friend We Have in Jesus" By Joseph Medlicott Scriven (1855)

1. What a friend we have in Jesus,
   all our sins and griefs to bear!
   What a privilege to carry
   everything to God in prayer!
   O what peace we often forfeit,
   O what needless pain we bear,
   all because we do not carry
   everything to God in prayer!

2. Have we trials and temptations?
   Is there trouble anywhere?
   We should never be discouraged;
   take it to the Lord in prayer!
   Can we find a friend so faithful
   who will all our sorrows share?
   Jesus knows our every weakness;
   take it to the Lord in prayer!

61

3. Are we weak and heavy laden,

cumbered with a load of care?

Precious Savior, still our refuge--

take it to the Lord in prayer!

Do your friends despise, forsake you?

Take it to the Lord in prayer!

In his arms he'll take and shield you;

you will find a solace there.

BE OPEN WITH GOD

Brother/sister, the Lord wants us to be as plain and truthful with Him and all those He will send our ways to help and guide us. When Hannah cried out, she received her miracle even though she was misjudged (1 Samuel 1:9-18). It was better that the Samaritan woman was plain and truthful with Jesus because she later realized that Jesus knew EVERYTHING about her.

"Jesus said to her, "Go, call your husband, and come here." The woman answered and said, "I have no husband." Jesus said to her, "You have well said, 'I have no husband,' for you have had five husbands, and the one whom you now have is not your husband; in that you spoke truly." But the hour is coming, and now is, when the true worshipers will worship the Father in spirit and truth; for the Father is seeking such to worship Him. God is Spirit, and those who worship Him must worship in spirit and truth" (John 4:16-18, 23-24 NKJV). May God help us to be honest in our dealings with Him and others, in the name of Jesus. Amen!

When we do eye service, pretending to be Christians only when we are in the church, and we are something else the rest of the week, God sees and knows EVERYTHING (He is Omniscient). He wants us to serve Him faithfully. Remember that He sees and knows EVERYTHING about us.

63

"Before I formed you in the womb, I knew you; Before you were born, I sanctified you; I ordained you a prophet to the nations" (Jeremiah 1:5 NKJV).

If someone knows us before we were formed, what is it about us that He doesn't know? Come out of your hiding place! Come just as you are. No matter the "veil" we put on, He can see clearly through them. He knows and sees it all. Give Him the chance to take it off and cover you with His Glory. Come with your pain, your wounded heart, with your crushed spirit. Come with ANY form of issues you may be having. Come to Jesus today, like the woman with the issue of blood and be determined to touch the hem of His garment.

"For she said to herself, 'If only I may touch His garment, I shall be made well'" (Matthew 9:21 NKJV). What a determination!

We may want to be open, but the "crowd" may be the obstacle or barrier disturbing us from getting through to Jesus. Dear brother/sister, kindly ignore the crowd, the noise, the discouragements, your past that you are not proud of or ANYTHING standing in your way or distracting you from touching the hem of His garment. Kindly allow God to remove the obstacles preventing you from reaching your goals. It is time to **Push Your Way Through the Crowd!** You can do it. Keep striving and pushing. You are almost there; you can't afford to give up now. You have gone this far by grace. The One who has been carrying and supporting you is still alive. He wants to help you. Come and receive your blessings, your healing, your deliverance, break through and all that you need to live a blessed, victorious and a fulfilled life, in the name of Jesus. Amen! YES, YOU CAN DO IT! You may be tired and discouraged. DON'T GIVE UP, PLEASE! Keep on pushing. The Lord is with you. *"But those who wait on the LORD, shall renew their strength; They shall mount up with wings like eagles, they shall run and not be weary, they shall walk and not faint"* (Isaiah 40:31 NKJV). Victory is yours, in the mighty name of Jesus. Amen!

Sometimes, the enemy wants us to feel as if our failures are so great. He tries to give us the wrong impression that we have been condemned and we cannot be forgiven and that we are so filthy to approach God's throne of grace. He tries to make us feel so ashamed and unworthy to be in the crowd, most especially when we have accepted the label the world has given us— "UNCLEAN." We need to learn to be like the woman with the issue of blood. She was regarded as "unclean" because of her condition (the blood issue). For more understanding about body fluids (semen/blood) and what the Bible calls unclean, read Leviticus 15:1-33. Despite the impression and the label, she had the grace to ignore the crowd, and she was DETERMINED to reach out and touch the hem of Jesus' garment.

"Now a woman, having a flow of blood for twelve years, who had spent all her livelihood on physicians and could not be healed by any, came from behind and touched the border of His garment. And immediately her flow of blood stopped. And Jesus said, "Who

65

touched Me?" When all denied it, Peter and those with him said, "Master, the multitudes throng and press You, and You say, 'Who touched Me?' But Jesus said, "Somebody touched Me, for I perceived power going out from Me." Now when the woman saw that she was not hidden, she came trembling; and falling down before Him, she declared to Him in the presence of all the people the reason she had touched Him and how she was healed immediately. And He said to her, "Daughter, be of good cheer; your faith has made you well. Go in peace"
(Luke 8:43-48 NKJV).

I don't know how long you have been dealing with condemnations of all kinds—unclean, unworthy, unlovable and so on. Only God knows how long your heart has been bleeding; He knows how hard you have been trying to climb that "mountain" that seems so insurmountable. Darling child of God, I have no clue about the "crowd" surrounding you, preventing you from receiving your deliverance. I can only encourage you to reach out and touch the hem of His garment. Come out of your hiding place. It is time to bow before Him and receive your healing. Be of good cheer, darling brother/sister. You shall overcome. Come to the fountain filled with blood that is drawn from Immanuel's veins. Let it take away your guilt and wash all my sins away. May the good Lord forgive us of our sins, heal us of our "infirmities," renew our souls, body, and mind, in the mighty name of Jesus. Amen! **DO NOT GIVE UP, PLEASE!**

Song of Meditation "There is A Fountain Filled with Blood"
By William Cowper (1772)

1. There is a fountain filled with blood.

Drawn from Immanuel's veins;

And sinners, plunged beneath that flood,

Lose all their guilty stains:

Lose all their guilty stains,

Lose all their guilty stains;

And sinners, plunged beneath that flood,

Lose all their guilty stains.

2. The dying thief rejoiced to see

That fountain in his day;

And there may I, though vile as he,

Wash all my sins away:

Wash all my sins away,

Wash all my sins away;

And there may I, though vile as he,

Wash all my sins away.

3. Dear dying Lamb, Thy precious blood

Shall never lose its pow'r,

Till all the ransomed Church of God

Be saved, to sin no more:

Be saved, to sin no more,

Be saved, to sin no more;

Till all the ransomed Church of God

Be saved to sin no more.

4. E'er since by faith I saw the stream

Thy flowing wounds supply,

Redeeming love has been my theme,

And shall be till I die:

And shall be till I die,

And shall be till I die;

Redeeming love has been my theme,

And shall be till I die.

5. When this poor lisping, stamm'ring tongue

Lies silent in the grave,

Then in a nobler, sweeter song

I'll sing Thy pow'r to save:

I'll sing Thy pow'r to save,

I'll sing Thy pow'r to save;

Then in a nobler, sweeter song

I'll sing Thy pow'r to save.

Prayer

Dear heavenly Father, I bless Your Holy name on behalf of Your precious child reading this book at this time. Your child is tired, in need of Your grace and strength. Prevent him/her from giving up. Renew his/her strength and grant him/her the grace to be able to mount up with wings like eagles. May he/she never grow weary or faint. Nothing will hinder him/her from touching the hem of Your garment today, in the name of Jesus. May he/she be honest in his/her dealings with You and other people You have sent/will send to help him/her. Grant him/her the grace to receive the "living water that will 'quench' his/her "thirst," in the name of Jesus. Restore health, relationships, finances and other needs. I don't know this, Your child, but You do. I pray You meet his/her needs according to Your riches in glory, in the mighty name of Jesus. Amen!

WHEN JESUS STOOPS DOWN

S ome of us are exhausted from the weight of guilt the enemy put on us. Not only that; you might have been caught doing what you were not supposed to do. It may be that you are moving with the wrong crowd and the "Pharisees" in your life, who have been waiting for the chance to ridicule you, now have the opportunity to expose you and tarnish your name or get rid of you. It may look like the "crowd" is about to "stone" you. You may be saying within you, "Father, in your hands I commit my life," thinking you are about to die. Get this straight today: When you are in the presence of God, the host of heaven is with you (HALLELUJAH!) surrounding you with a "wall of fire." You are UNTOUCHABLE, darling child of God. You are safe and secure, in the name of Jesus. Amen!

It is written: *"Then the scribes and Pharisees brought to Him a woman caught in adultery. And when they had set her in the midst, they said to Him, "Teacher, this woman was caught in adultery, in the very act. Now Moses, in the law, commanded us that such should be stoned. But what do You say?" This they said, testing Him, that they might have something of which to accuse Him. But Jesus stooped down and wrote on the ground with His finger, as though He did not hear"* (John 8:3-6 NKJV). Let your focus be on God, not your accusers. They are "toothless bulldogs." Allow God to fight your battle.

"So when they continued asking Him, He raised Himself up and said to them, "He who is without sin among you, let him throw a stone at her first." And again, He stooped down and wrote on the ground. Then those who heard it, being convicted by their conscience, went out one by one, beginning with the oldest even to the last. And Jesus was left alone, and the woman standing in the midst" (John 8:7-9 NKJV).

Darling child of God, Jesus has "stooped down," with His great power and authority on your behalf, disarming your enemy, making them drop the "stones" or any form of "weapon" or evidence/s they want to use against you, rendering them powerless. When Jesus "stoops down," enemies are bound to disappear from your presence. He is ready to come down to your level and lift you up from the hands of your accusers, from anxiety, depression and all that may be disturbing you from living a fulfilled life. He died on the cross of Calvary to make your life worth living. My darling brother/sister in the Lord, Jesus is at the door. Kindly let Him in.

With the Lord on your side, you are more than a conqueror, in the mighty name of Jesus. Amen!

If Jesus has not condemned you, why are you worried about the accusations, condemnations or "stigma?" It is written, *"When Jesus had raised Himself up and saw no one but the woman, He said to her, "Woman, where are those accusers of yours? Has no one condemned you?" She said, "No one, Lord." And Jesus said* to her, *"neither do I condemn you; go and sin no more."* Then *Jesus spoke to them again, saying, "I am the light of the world. He who follows Me shall not walk in darkness, but have the light of life"* (John 8:10-12 NKJV). May God grant you the grace to ignore the "crowd" and the "noise." May you receive your healing/deliverance today, may you follow the "light of the world" and NEVER have to walk in darkness anymore, in the mighty name of Jesus. Amen!

Song of Meditation "He Came Down to My Level" By Dwight Liles/Gaither Vocal Band

LET IT OUT

Things can get so overwhelming at times, and we may need that special, devoted and trustworthy friend to talk to. Bottling things up for too long is not good for the body, soul or mind. Unfortunately, because of fear of ridicule, insults, name-calling and other negative things that may come out of it, it is very sad to say that it could be very difficult to show the "REAL FACE" (i.e., to share our burdens with people). We doubt that they will be able to help or fear that they will make matters worse. There are some "wonderful," "holier than thou" Christians who have made themselves lawyers/judges without any law degree. They will judge you and try to make you feel like a bad Christian if you let them. Some may even stop talking to you. They may start treating you like a sinner or an ingrate.

They will remind you of all that God has done for you, most especially those things they are yet to receive from God, and they are too much in a hurry to wait for their own time, and they may be ashamed to confess that they are envious of you. We are all children of God. He has promised to bless us all. We just need to wait for our own time, appreciate the gifts He has given us and stop envying others and thinking that the grass is greener on the other side of the fence. Let us water and nurture the "grass" in our own yard and see how green and attractive it will turn out. Remember that we are "wired" differently. It is written: *"And He*

Himself gave some to be apostles, some prophets, some evangelists, and some pastors and teachers"
(Ephesians 4:11 NKJV).

Talking to the jealous ones may make matters worse. They may add "salt and pepper" to your story and make it more complicated. THERE IS GOD, OOOH! (laugh with me). He sees and knows it all. You may hear them say, "If I were you, I would do A, B, C, D." REMEMBER; they are not you, and they may not have any good intentions. It is okay for people to advise you. Just do not forget that you will be responsible for your action/s. I am telling you today that the people judging you are a bunch of "liars," not "lawyers," because what they may be telling you may be contrary to what God is telling you. Whom do you want to continue to listen to? "Liars" or the lover of your soul (Jesus)? He came into the world **NOT** to condemn, but that the world through Him might be saved (John 3:17). "Burdens are lifted at Calvary; brother/sister in the Lord. Jesus is ALWAYS there." Allow Him to take the "heavy load" from you today.

There is an adage in Yoruba that says: It is impossible to walk and have your head erect without moving or shaking. It means that we are bound to make mistakes. This is the same as trying to avoid meeting these "wonderful" people as we travel along the "wilderness journey." Unfortunately, we will encounter them almost EVERYWHERE we go in life—at home, work, school, even in the church. The point is: Don't be discouraged when you cross paths with them. You just have to know the extent to which you let them into your life. One Yoruba adage says visitors who belong in your living room are to remain there. They have no business knowing the way to your "bedroom." This I will call UNNECESSARY EXPOSURE! While we are waiting patiently to receive the discerning spirit from God, and the "tempest" is still high, may our Savior hide us till the storm of life is over. We commit our helpless souls onto Him as we patiently wait on His grace to send us the trustworthy people we can talk to. May we be that "special" someone to somebody as well. May God's grace cover our "wounds" and revive our "fainting" souls, in the mighty name of Jesus. Amen!

Song of Meditation "Jesus, Lover of my Soul" By Charles Wesley (1740)

1. Jesus, lover of my soul,

Let me to Thy bosom fly,

While the nearer waters roll,

While the tempest still is high:

Chorus

Hide me, O my Savior, hide,

Till the storm of life is past;

Safe into the haven guide;

O receive my soul at last.

2. Other refuge have I none,

Hangs my helpless soul on Thee;

Leave, oh, leave me not alone,

Still support and comfort me.

3. All my trust in Thee is stayed,

All my help from Thee I bring;

Cover my defenseless head

With the shadow of Thy wing.

4. Thou, O Christ, art all I want;

More than all in Thee I find;

Raise the fallen, cheer the faint,

Heal the sick and lead the blind.

5. Just and holy is Thy name,

I am all unrighteousness;

Vile and full of sin I am,

Thou art full of truth and grace.

6. Plenteous grace with Thee is found,

Grace to cover all my sin;

Let the healing streams abound;

Make and keep me pure within.

7. Thou of life the fountain art,

Freely let me take of Thee;

Spring Thou up within my heart,

Rise to all eternity.

JESUS IS PASSING

There is no doubt that everyone needs somebody. I might have said this many times already, but this truth bears repeating. We may not be able to tell who people truly are just by looking at their faces. May we be directed to the true and faithful ones who will help lighten our burdens and not add to them, in the name of Jesus. Amen! Take off the "makeup/veil" and show your "real face" because Jesus is passing. You are not reading this book now by accident. God is telling you today that He wants to help and set you free from WHATEVER may be making you feel down, dejected, unloved, unwanted or from ANYTHING that is stealing your joy. Show your "real face," cry out for His mercy and let him heal you today, in the name of Jesus. It is written: *"And behold, two blind men sitting by the road, when they heard that Jesus was passing by, cried out, saying, "Have mercy on us, O Lord, Son of David"* (Matthew 20:30 NKJV)! No matter where you are "sitting" now, do not miss this opportunity, darling child of God. Lift up your voice in faith and cry out to Jesus to have mercy on you. It is time to get up from the "sitting" position. Get up in faith and receive your healing, in the mighty name of Jesus. Amen!

It is written: *"Then the multitude warned them that they should be quiet; but they cried out all the more, saying, "Have mercy on us, O Lord, Son of David!" So Jesus stood still and called them,* and said, *"What do you want Me to do for you?" They said to Him, "Lord, that our eyes may be opened." So Jesus had compassion and touched their eyes. And immediately their eyes received sight, and they followed Him"* (Matthew 20:31-34 NKJV). Here comes the multitude/crowd again. The treatment remains the same: IGNORE THEM! Just answer the question Jesus is asking you: **"WHAT DO YOU WANT ME TO DO FOR YOU?"** The blind men requested for their sights to be restored. It was recorded that Jesus had compassion for them, touched their eyes, and their sights were restored IMMEDIATELY. Darling brother/sister, it is written: *"Through the LORD's mercies we are not consumed, because His compassions fail not. They are new every morning; great is Your faithfulness"* (Lamentations 3:22-23 NKJV). Hallelujah! May God have mercy on all of us, hear our cries, restore our sights, health, family and ALL that needs to be restored in our lives. May He answer our prayers as we call on His holy name today and ALWAYS, in the name of Jesus. Amen!

Song of Meditation "Jesus is Passing, Jesus is Passing" By Franklin E. Belden (1886)

1. Jesus is passing, Jesus is passing,

Come, all ye blind, and receive now your sight;

He will bend o'er you,

He will restore you,

He will exchange all your darkness for light;

78

Come, and the Savior will give you your sight.

2. Jesus is passing, Jesus is passing,

Come now, ye lame, to the Healer of all;

His life He gave you,

One look will save you,

He will attend to the poor cripple's call;

Now He is passing, is passing for all.

3. Jesus is passing, Jesus is passing,

Come, all ye poor, to the plenteous store;

Now He will lead you,

Ever will feed you;

Jesus invites you to hunger no more;

Come to the bountiful heavenly store.

4. Jesus is passing, Jesus is passing,

Come, ye afflicted by sin and by shame;

O we implore you,

Let Him restore you;

Come while He lingers and calls you by name;

Come, all ye laden with sin and with shame.

PRAYER IS THE MASTER KEY!

R ight where you are reading this book, take a moment and talk to your heavenly Father about your concerns. It is written: *"Ask, and it will be given to you; seek, and you will find; knock, and it will be opened to you. For everyone who asks receives, and he who seeks finds, and to him who knocks it will be opened"* (Matthew 7:7-8 NKJV). When you kneel down in the presence of God in prayer, He will SURELY stand up and fight for you. When He stands up for you, your enemies and their agents can NEVER stand against you. I tell you, if you kneel before God, you can stand before ANYONE, including kings. Do not be surprised to find yourself in the WHITE HOUSE (laugh with me). Darling brother/sister in the Lord, it is time to pray.

Tell Him all your heart's desires and let Him perfect His will in your life. People might have disappointed you, betrayed your trust, and you have "recoiled" completely back into your "shell." You are finding it so difficult to trust and love again. You have built an "invisible wall" to prevent people from coming close to you. You don't want anyone to hurt you anymore. The Lord is calling you out of your "shell" today. He will NEVER fail you. He wants to spend time with you. Give ALL the hurts, the pains/aches and ALL that is disturbing you to Him. Pour your heart out to Him. My brother/sister, prayer, is the "master key" that unlocks the doors of blessings the enemy has closed, and it seals all the negative doors that God Himself has closed in our lives, with the blood of Jesus. They will be closed PERMANENTLY in His holy name. Furthermore, the "doors" of healing, prosperity, promotion and other blessings from above that God has opened will remain open, and NO ONE will be able to close them on you, in the name of Jesus.

WHOEVER tries to reverse any of the above mentioned will have his/her "hand caught in the door," in the mighty name of Jesus. When Jesus says YES or NO, NO ONE can say the opposite. When He lifts you up, NO ONE can pull you down. You might have been lost in sin, and the weight is weighing you down, robbing you of your joy and peace. Bear in mind: Jesus has paid ALL your "debts" in full with His precious blood, on the cross of Calvary. He has forgiven and accepted you just as you are. It is time for you to let the light of glory from heaven fill your soul. Allow Him to bathe your heart in His AMAZING love. All you need to do is just have a little talk with Jesus, our Savior, Redeemer and Friend and let Him make EVERYTHING right for you. It is time to receive your "sight/blessings." ALL that God has done for you will be PERMANENT, in the mighty name of Jesus. Amen!

Song of Meditation "Prayer is The Key" By Unknown Artiste

Prayer is the key,

Prayer is the key,

Prayer is the master key.

Jesus started with prayer.

And ended with prayer.

Prayer is the master key.

Song of Meditation "Just a Little Talk with Jesus" By Cleavant Derricks

Song of Meditation "He is A Miracle Working God" By Unknown Artiste

He is a miracle, working God,

He is a miracle, working God,

He is the Alpha and Omega,

He is A Miracle, working God.

WHAT HAVE I DONE, LORD?

H ave you or people around you ever asked if your challenges are due to the sins you or someone in your family has committed? Darling brother/sister in the Lord, it is not about you or about ANYONE in your family. It is ALL about God. Some of us, calling ourselves Christians, have serious issues, sorry to say. We are quick to attribute challenges or illnesses (even death) to sin or something someone has done. It is written: *"And His disciples asked Him, saying, "Rabbi, who sinned, this man or his parents, that he was born blind"* (John 9:2 NKJV). It is easy to listen to the lies of the enemy that you are going through trials because of your "sins." Fellow believers may even challenge you with this same question: Who sinned? Kindly remind them that it is written: *"We all have sinned and fall short of the glory of God"* (Romans 3:23). Tell them that we are ALL sinners. It is written: *"Behold, I was brought forth in iniquity, and in sin my mother conceived me"* (Psalm 51:5 NKJV). May God forgive and help us all, in the mighty name of Jesus. Amen!

Darling child of God, it is written: *"If You, LORD, should mark iniquities, O Lord, who could stand"* (Psalm 130:3 NKJV). Lord have mercy! It is written: *"Yes, and all who desire to live godly in Christ Jesus will suffer persecution"* (2 Timothy 3:12 NKJV). I have been told several times: You are always praying, singing and surrounding yourself with the word of God. Look at your life.

Some even told me it was because of the way they have cursed me. They have forgotten that no one can curse those whom God has not cursed nor denounce those whom the LORD has not denounced (Numbers 23:8). Hallelujah! I totally agree that I am a sinner, but what did Jesus do to deserve the agony He went through for our sins? He NEVER sinned. It is written: *"For we do not have a high priest who cannot sympathize with our weaknesses, but was in all points tempted as we are, yet without sin"* (Hebrews 4:15 NKJV). *"For He made Him who knew no sin to be sin for us, that we might become the righteousness of God in Him"* (2 Corinthians 5:21 NKJV).

The Bible says we were born in sin. Notwithstanding, let it be known that your challenges are not due to your sins or anything anyone has done. God is up to something good in your life. Hold on, and don't let go. You will soon testify of God's goodness, in the name of Jesus. It is written: *"But may the God of all grace, who called us to His eternal glory by Christ Jesus, after you have suffered a while, perfect, establish, strengthen, and settle you"* (1 Peter 5:10 NKJV). The Bible says, *"For our light affliction, which is but for a moment, is working for us a far more exceeding and eternal weight of glory"* (2 Corinthians 4:17 NKJV). *"I now rejoice in my sufferings for you, and fill up in my flesh what is lacking in the afflictions of Christ, for the sake of His body, which is the church"* (Colossians 1:24 NKJV). God wants to use your "ISSUES" to glorify His name. Your suffering will not be in vain.

AMAZING testimonies will come out of it, in the mighty name of Jesus. Amen!

WHO GAVE THE CONSENT?

There was no record of any sin committed by Job. He had his own trials. God trusted that he would not disappoint Him. God does not need our permission to direct our lives the way He wishes. Notwithstanding, He promised that he will not tempt us more than what we can bear. It is written: *"There was a man in the land of Uz, whose name was Job; and that man was blameless and upright, and one who feared God and shunned evil"* (Job 1:1 NKJV). A man who feared God and shunned evil was severely tested. It is very interesting to know that God Himself gave Satan the "consent" to try Job. It is written: *"Now there was a day when the sons of God came to present themselves before the LORD, and Satan also came among them. And the LORD said to Satan, "From where do you come?" So, Satan answered the LORD and said, "From going to and fro on the earth, and from walking back and forth on it. "Then the LORD said to Satan, "Have you considered My servant Job, that there is none like him on the earth, a blameless and upright man, one who fears God and shuns evil?" So, Satan answered the LORD and said, "Does Job fear God for nothing? Have You not made a hedge around him, around his household, and around all that he has on every side? You have blessed the work of his hands, and his possessions have increased in the land. But now, stretch out Your hand and touch all that he has, and he will surely curse You to Your face!"*

And the LORD said to Satan, "Behold, all that he has is in your power; only do not lay a hand on his person." So, Satan went out from the presence of the LORD" (Job 1:6-12 NKJV). Lord have mercy! In one day, the enemy attacked Job so hard (Job 1:13-18).

Despite all the afflictions from the enemy, we were told that Job did not sin or charge God with wrong. It is written: *"Then Job arose, tore his robe, and shaved his head; and he fell to the ground and worshiped. And he said: "Naked I came from my mother's womb, and naked shall I return there. The LORD gave, and the LORD has taken away; Blessed be the name of the LORD." In all this Job did not sin nor charge God with wrong"* (Job 1:20-22 NKJV). The story did not end there. It is written: *"Now the LORD blessed the latter days of Job more than his beginning; for he had fourteen thousand sheep, six thousand camels, one thousand yoke of oxen, and one thousand female donkeys"* (Job 42:12 NKJV). I pray that your tomorrow will be greater than today, in the name of Jesus. All your mockers will become your workers. Almighty God will lift you up from grass to grace, you will be promoted from shame to fame, your story is about to change from zero to hero. I pray that all the insults you have received will yield results of greatness, and you will testify in the land of the living, in the mighty name of Jesus. Amen!

HIGHLY FAVORED

C ould it be that you are doing something "good" or pleasing to God, and He wants to give you a bigger assignment, and you must pass through "fire" for purification so that you will come out shining like gold? What was Mary's sin? It is written: *"Now in the sixth month the **ANGEL GABRIEL WAS SENT BY GOD** to a city of Galilee named Nazareth, to a virgin betrothed to a man whose name was Joseph, of the house of David. The virgin's name was Mary. And having come in, the angel said to her, "**REJOICE, HIGHLY FAVORED ONE**, the Lord is with you; blessed are you among women!" But when she saw him, she was troubled at his saying, and considered what manner of greeting this was. Then the angel said to her, "Do not be afraid, Mary, for you have found favor with God. And behold, you will conceive in your womb and bring forth a Son, and shall call His name JESUS. He will be great, and will be called the Son of the Highest; and the Lord God will give Him the throne of His father David. And He will reign over the house of Jacob forever, and of His kingdom there will be no end. "Then Mary said to the angel, "How can this be, since I do not know a man?" "And the angel answered and said to her, "The Holy Spirit will come upon you, and the power of the Highest will overshadow you; therefore, also, that Holy One who is to be born will be called the Son of God. Now indeed, Elizabeth your relative has also* *conceived a son in her old age; and this is now the sixth month for her who was called barren. For with God nothing will be impossible. "Then Mary said, "Behold the maidservant of the Lord! Let it be to me according to your word." And the angel departed from her"* (Luke 1:26-38 NKJV; emphasis added).

Let us take the highlighted part of the verses one by one: It was shown that Angel Gabriel was sent by God, not by any earthly king. Why Mary, amongst other virgins in Galilee? If God decides to use a virgin for His work, why not one who is not yet betrothed to a man? Mary's Immaculate Conception created friction between her and Joseph before Angel Gabriel finally explained the situation to Joseph. How would you have handled this case if you were to be in Joseph's shoes? It wouldn't have been farfetched for him to say, "Okay, lady, you cheated on me, and now you are telling me it was God's doing. Do you think I am a fool?" God is faithful about not tempting us more than we can handle. He knew He could depend on Joseph to support Mary and that he would easily believe the message. It is written: *"Now the birth of Jesus Christ was as follows: After His mother, Mary, was betrothed to Joseph, before they came together, she was found with child of the Holy Spirit. Then Joseph, her husband, being a just man **and not wanting to make her a public example, was minded to put her away secretly.** But while he thought about these things, behold, an angel of the Lord appeared to him in a dream, saying, "Joseph, son of David, do not be afraid to take to you*

Mary your wife, for that which is conceived in her is of the Holy Spirit" (Matthew 1:18-20 NKJV; emphasis added).

It was reported to Joseph: *"And she will bring forth a Son, and you shall call His name JESUS, for He will save His people from their sins." So, all this was done that it might be fulfilled which was spoken by the Lord through the prophet, saying: "Behold, the virgin shall be with child, and bear a Son, and they shall call His name Immanuel," which is translated, "God with us." Then Joseph, being aroused from sleep, did as the angel of the Lord commanded him and took to him his wife, and did not know her till she had brought forth her firstborn Son. And he called His name JESUS"* (Matthew 1:21-25 NKJV). May God depend on all of us and grant us the grace to protect our significant others from shame/ridicule or anything that will make the world insult or humiliate them, in the mighty name of Jesus. Amen!

Sometimes, God is silent and allows our challenging situations known to people before proving Himself? If an angel from God should appear to any of us today and say, "Rejoice, highly favored one, the Lord is with you; blessed are you among women/men!" How would you feel? I would feel on top of the world and be rest assured that I am in for the best. God does things differently in ways that ONLY He understands: It is written: *"For My thoughts are not your thoughts, nor are your ways My ways,"* says the LORD. *"For as the heavens are higher than the earth, so are My ways higher than your ways, and My thoughts than your thoughts"* (Isaiah 55:8-9 NKJV).

Who are we to question Him? Highly favored Mary, who was told that the Lord is with her and that she was blessed among women, had to travel to Bethlehem while she was close to delivery. There was no record of a luxurious limousine with an entourage noted in the report, no travel nurse in case of any emergency. It was a very rough trip! **OUCH!**

It is written: *"And it came to pass in those days that a decree went out from Caesar Augustus that all the world should be registered. This census first took place while Quirinius was governing Syria. So, all went to be registered, everyone to his own city. Joseph also went up from Galilee, out of the city of Nazareth, into Judea, to the city of David, which is called Bethlehem, because he was of the house and lineage of David, to be registered with Mary, his betrothed wife, who was with child. So it was, that while they were there, the days were completed for her to be delivered"* (Luke 2:1-6 NKJV). As if the rough and tiring trip was not enough, the "highly favored" had to give birth to the Messiah in a manger. It is written: *"So, it was, that while they were there, the days were completed for her to be delivered. And she brought forth her firstborn Son, and wrapped Him in swaddling clothes, and laid Him in a manger, because there was no room for them in the inn"* (Luke 2:6-7 NKJV).

As the mother of Jesus, the "HIGHLY FAVORED" one would think that she would have been registered in the best hospital in town and cared for by the best obstetrics and gynecologist, and that best pediatrician would take care of baby Jesus after birth.

Highly favored! Her son was crucified; He went through severe agony for the sins He did not commit, and she watched Him die on the cross between two thieves: It is written: *"Now there stood by the cross of Jesus His mother, and His mother's sister, Mary the wife of Clopas, and Mary Magdalene"* (John 19:25 NKJV). I don't know how "HIGHLY FAVORED" you are. I pray that the Lord will grant you the grace to be faithful to the end, in the mighty name of Jesus. Amen!

Darling brother/sister, let me quickly reinforce that; your challenges are not due to your sins or the sins of your parents or ancestors. God is allowing whatever you are going through to happen to you for His name to be glorified. Our God can deliver, and He will save us, in the mighty name of Jesus. Maybe you are in the "oven" or passing through the "fire" of life. I don't know the "degree" God has set the "oven" or how long the time He has set it for. I pray that you will come out "well done." You will come out shining like gold. May the good Lord replenish ALL that the enemy has taken away from you in many folds, in the name of Jesus. I pray that God will grant you the spirit of perseverance. May He uphold you with His right hand of righteousness. By His special grace, you will be able to stand firm, immovable and you will not sin against Him throughout this trying period, in the name of Jesus. Your testimony time is almost here, and it will be a full one, in the mighty name of Jesus. Amen! Hold on, and DON'T GIVE UP, PLEASE!

Prayer

Heavenly Father, I take this moment to commit all your children going through their challenges into your hands. Kindly grant us the grace to hold on tight to you and NEVER give up. I pray for the ladies who are pregnant outside of wedlock and facing all sorts of embarrassments. Kindly forgive them, and please provide them with "Josephs" that will help cover their "shame," in the name of Jesus. Grant them safe delivery, Father. I pray that you make yourself known in our situations before it is too late. I plead the blood of Jesus over our children, help them so that they will be signs and wonders that You have promised they will be. Make them head and not tail. May we NEVER have any reason to cry over them, in the name of Jesus. Amen! Heavenly Father, we are so proud of Job when we read about him in the Bible. We don't want to go through what he went through, Lord. Whatever we go through in life, we know that You will be there ALL the way to guide and support us. Help us so that we will not sin against You, in the mighty name of Jesus. *"Let the words of our mouths and the meditation of our hearts; Be acceptable in Your sight, o LORD, our strength and my Redeemer"* (Psalm 19:14). Father, help us to surrender EVERYTHING about us to you and to trust your leading, in the mighty name of Jesus. Amen!

Song of Meditation "All to Jesus I Surrender" By Judson W. Van De Venter (1896)

1. All to Jesus I surrender,

All to Him I freely give;

I will ever love and trust Him,

In His presence daily live.

Chorus

I surrender all,

I surrender all.

All to Thee, my blessed Savior,

I surrender all.

2. All to Jesus I surrender,

Humbly at His feet I bow,

Worldly pleasures all forsaken;

Take me, Jesus, take me now.

3. All to Jesus I surrender,

Make me, Savior, wholly Thine;

Let me feel Thy Holy Spirit,

Truly know that Thou art mine.

4. All to Jesus I surrender,

Lord, I give myself to Thee;

Fill me with Thy love and power,

Let Thy blessing fall on me.

5. All to Jesus I surrender,

Now I feel the sacred flame.

Oh, the joy of full salvation!

Glory, glory to His name!

JUDGE NOT

As God is wiping our tears away, exalting our valleys and leveling our "mountains" and "hills," may He grant us the grace to meet with people who will not use our past/present issues to judge us, in the name of Jesus. Amen! May God direct us to those who will be interested in being their brothers' and sisters' keepers. May we all be filled with acts of caring and loving. May these wonderful attributes be manifested in us anywhere we go, in the name of Jesus. Amen! How many of our friends, neighbors, husbands, wives, siblings, students, coworkers or church members have we turned to the "valley" of depression by judging them and making them feel bad about themselves for sharing their concerns with us? How many people have committed suicide in the process? Lord have mercy!

When you tell some people your story, all they want to do is judge you. They assess you based on your academic achievements, financial and other status that matters to them. The level of your pain may not really be of any concern at all, most especially if you don't belong to a certain "class." If you kindly forgive me, I will say, "At times, money talks, if not all the time." When you have no money, and you don't know whose you are (a child of God), some people would like to treat you like "garbage," that is, if you let them. It is important for us to know our worth.

I had an experience where I had to share my concerns with someone, trusting that the person will be able to counsel in a godly manner. There are recommendations in the Bible on how to settle quarrels or misunderstandings. It is written: *"Moreover, if your brother sins against you, go and tell him his fault between you and him alone. If he hears you, you have gained your brother. But if he will not hear, take with you one or two more, that 'by the mouth of two or three witnesses every word may be established.' And if he refuses to hear them, tell it to the church. But if he refuses even to hear the church, let him be to you like a heathen and a tax collector"* (Matthew 18:15-17 NKJV).

I tried to follow this recommendation, only to experience disappointment. As I have written before and may still come up as you read along: We all have issues, and everyone needs someone. I had an "issue" one day (laugh with me), and it was beyond what I thought I could handle by myself. So, I made the mistake of "running" to the phone instead of "running" to the throne of God. When I expressed my concerns, the person did not believe me. The responses to what I reported made me feel like I was lying. What really broke the camel's back was when the person said, "Do you know the position these people hold in society?" I was highly disappointed. It was like the challenges and the negative effect this unresolved issue might cause were not important. The message I received and the way it was perceived that day was, "Lady, you are not important, you have no fame nor position in the society, and I am not ready to jeopardize my relationship with the ones you are concerned about. I was terribly upset.

If not for God, things like this may be damaging, and one may not be able to handle this lightly. I quickly remembered one of the nursing diagnoses: "Knowledge deficit." I told myself; this person was unable to see the "ROYALTY" in me (laugh with me). Apparently, he didn't recognize that I am a princess, the child of the Most High God. So, I had to reintroduce myself. I said, "Do you know the position I hold in the kingdom of God? Do you know that I am the daughter of the King of kings, Lord of lords, the All-knowing Father?" I quickly reminded this person RESPECTFULLY that I am precious to God, fearfully and wonderfully made. I tell you, I was not afraid to "speak the word" because the Lord did not give me the spirit of fear. Neither has He given it to you. It is written: *"For God has not given us a spirit of fear, but of power and of love and of a sound mind"*
(2 Timothy 1:7 NKJV).

It was a learning opportunity for both of us that day. Darling brother/sister, you really must know your worth in the Lord and not allow people to toss you around. Your "weight" in the Lord must not be too light for any form of "wind" to blow you away. Be "solid" in Him. Lack of money or position should NOT change your name, just that the world may not add any "title" to it. So what? If you don't know, let me tell you that you are a prince/princess, and you mean the whole world to God. The world may call it "pride;" I call it knowing your worth in Christ! You may need to rewrite your "resume" if you have forgotten who you are, what you mean to God, and all the qualifications He has given you. Just a quick reminder, brother/sister in the Lord, you are LOADED!

The case presented to this individual was not as complicated or as challenging as the one King Solomon had to deal with, but this particular person was judging based on the status of the people involved in the dispute. If not for God, I could have felt so bad, discouraged and depressed because of this individual's attitude I trusted for resolution, who turned out to be a very bad "lawyer"— one who judges without facts and God's guidance. It would be very nice if all of us could stay away from judging others, more so if we don't know the whole story. If we cannot take people's burdens away, we should not add to them, please! We can pray with people if we can't help in any other way or just listen. One of the important communication skills is listening. So, darling brother/sister, do not jump to conclusions and please, DO NOT JUDGE!

One Yoruba adage says: "If we have not passed through a road or street during broad daylight and be able to master all the areas with potholes, dangerous pits or other life-threatening things along that road, it may be very dangerous to travel that path at night because one can easily fall into any of these dangers." If we must go through that "route," we know to do it with care. It is the same with conflict resolution. Hear both sides and seek God's counsel. It is written: *"Test all things; hold fast what is good.*

Abstain from every form of evil. Now may the God of peace Himself sanctify you completely; and may your whole spirit, soul, and body be preserved blameless at the coming of our Lord Jesus Christ" (Thessalonians 5:21-23 NKJV). Amen!

If there is a need to make any form of "judgment," let us pray to God for uncommon wisdom like He gave to Solomon in the Bible (1 Kings 3:16-28), when He was faced with the challenging case of two women with a living and one dead child. God helped him make a wise judgment by giving the living child to the real mother: You can imagine the chaos if the living child was given to the wrong mother. It is written: *"Now two women who were harlots came to the king, and stood before him. And one woman said, "O my lord, this woman and I dwell in the same house; and I gave birth while she was in the house. Then it happened, the third day after I had given birth, that this woman also gave birth. And we were together; no one was with us in the house, except the two of us in the house. And this woman's son died in the night, because she lay on him. So, she arose in the middle of the night and took my son from my side, while your maidservant slept, and laid him in her bosom, and laid her dead child in my bosom. And when I rose in the morning to nurse my son, there he was, dead. But when I had examined him in the morning, indeed, he was not my son whom I had borne"* (1 Kings 3:16-21).

The story continues thus: *"Then the other woman said, "No! But the living one is my son, and the dead one is your son." And the first woman said, "No! But the dead one is your son, and the living one is my son." Thus, they spoke before the king. And the king said, "The one says, this is my son, who lives, and your son is the dead one; and the other says, 'No! But your son is the dead one, and my son is the living one." Then the king said, "Bring me a sword." So, they brought a sword before the king. And the king said, "Divide the living child in two, and give half to one, and half to the other." Then the woman whose son was living spoke to the king, for she yearned with compassion for her son; and she said, "O my lord, give her the living child, and by no means kill him!" But the other said, "Let him be neither mine nor yours, but divide him." So, the king answered and said, "Give the first woman the living child, and by no means kill him; she is his mother." And all Israel heard of the judgment which the king had rendered; and they feared the king, for they saw that the wisdom of God was in him to administer justice* (1 Kings 3:22-28 NKJV). Thank God for the UNCOMMON wisdom.

Unfortunately, when people know they are in a mess, they want to pull you along. Instead of protecting you from making the same mistake, they will try everything to drag you into their mess. When they see that they are going down, they want to pull you down as well. This is what I call "first class wickedness." May God help us not to fall victim, in the mighty name of Jesus. Amen! The God of Solomon, the giver of knowledge, wisdom and understanding is still alive, and He is willing to give us the uncommon wisdom we need if we don't allow money, position/fame, manipulation or hearing one side of the story, blindfold us into making wrong "judgments." We are to remind ourselves that we are going to "judge the angels." It is written:

"Do you not know that we shall judge angels? How much more, things that pertain to this life" (1 Corinthians 6:3)? Tell me, which of the law schools in this world will teach us how to judge the angels when we can't even judge ourselves? It is ONLY through the help of God and for us to COMPLETELY surrender to Him. There is no other way of acquiring this "special" and "divine" knowledge. We better be very careful. If the angels will be judged, what will happen to us, who were born in sin? May God help us all, in the mighty name of Jesus. Amen!

As Christians, especially leaders, we are EVERYTHING to our families, our churches and the community. The church is our courtroom, emergency room and classroom where we learn more about God and people. Moreover, it is supposed to be a shelter in the time of "storm." As leaders, the Lord has put us in charge, and He wants us to represent Him. Therefore, we must operate through His divine guidance. We cannot rely on our own understanding. It is written: *"Trust in the LORD with all your heart, and lean not on your own understanding; In all your ways acknowledge Him, and He shall direct your paths"* (Proverbs 3:5-6 NKJV).

Growing up, my father had the opportunity to counsel as a pastor in Nigeria and most of the people he counseled expressed gratitude to the glory of God. Some kings, chiefs, governors and people of all tribes and cultures came to him for counsel, and he

101

was able to help many. Some of our leaders and pastors are playing it very safe these days due to the culture and fear of litigation problems. This should not be the case. With God's help, we can BOLDLY say things the way they are by applying God's given wisdom. May He grant us the grace to be able to say the most unpleasant things in the most pleasant ways, in the name of Jesus. It is written: *"If any of you lacks wisdom, let him ask of God, who gives to all liberally and without reproach, and it will be given to him"* (James 1:5 NKJV). ***"The fear of the LORD is the beginning of knowledge."*** (Proverbs 1:7; emphasis added). May God help us to "fear" Him accordingly and not compromise in any way, in the mighty name of Jesus. Amen!

For those of us who are praying to God for UNCOMMON wisdom, to the leaders at home, churches and businesses, in our countries or anywhere we find ourselves as leaders, God is ready to work with us if we let Him. I pray against the misuse of power for our leaders. May there be peace, love, unity and safety wherever we find ourselves as leaders, in the mighty name of Jesus. Amen! In addition, we are to remember that everything is about STEWARDSHIP! We are going to give an account of EVERYTHING and no condition is permanent! Let us try as much as possible to start building a positive legacy from day one of our services. It is written: *"A good name is better than precious ointment, and the day of death than the day of one's birth"* (Ecclesiastes 7:1 NKJV).

"The memory of the righteous is blessed, but the name of the wicked will rot"
(Proverbs 10:7 NKJV).

BE A BLESSING NOT A PROBLEM/PAIN

When we are going through challenges, some of us may become so bitter and may want to act out of revenge. This happens especially when we have been hurt so bad. It is consistent with the popular saying: "You can only give what you have." As children of God, we have Christ living in us, whether we are on the "mountain" or in the "valley." We can still bless others who are on their own "battlefields," despite the pains and aches we may be experiencing. I plead that we choose not to be any form of pain or problem to others, even those who have hurt us. May our prayers for them be, *"Father forgive them, for they know not what they are doing"* (Luke 23:34). May God help us all to be what He wants us to be for Him. May He heal our wounds and grant us the grace to trade our sorrow for the joy of the Lord, in the mighty name of Jesus. Amen!

It is a great blessing to have someone to share your burdens and joys with—someone with good listening ears. As Christians, we have been instructed to look out for one another's wellbeing. We are to be our brother's/sister's keeper. It is written: *"Therefore comfort each other and edify one another, just as you also are doing"* (1 Thessalonians 5:11 NKJV). We need one another in this "wilderness journey." When one is weak, the strong ones should rally around and support the weak so that he or she does not fall, fail, break down or be put to shame. We are God's ears to listen to one another; His mouthpiece to speak words of kindness, encouragement, courage and comfort. We are His hands to embrace and carry one another during challenging times; His bank account to support one another financially. Additionally, I cannot overemphasize the importance of intercessory prayers, standing in the gap and presenting one another to the throne of grace. God will not come down from heaven. We are His EVERYTHING!

It is written: "*Then behold, men brought on a bed a man who was paralyzed, whom they sought to bring in and lay before Him. And when they could not find how they might bring him in, because of the crowd, they went up on the housetop and let him down with his bed through the tiling into the midst before Jesus. When He saw their faith, He said to him, "Man, your sins are forgiven you"* (Luke 5:18-20 NKJV). May God make all of us this kind of reliable, dependable, loving and caring friend, who will go to ANY length to be supportive of his/her friends and may He bless us with friends like them too, friends closer than a brother, in the name of Jesus. Amen! It is written: "*A man who has friends must himself be friendly, but there is a friend who sticks closer than a brother*" (Proverbs 18:24 NKJV). It is written: "*And the King will answer and say to them, 'Assuredly, I say to you, inasmuch as you did it to one of the least of these my brethren, you did it to me*" (Matthew 25:40 NKJV).

Are we ready to be our brother/sister's keeper, rescuing the perishing and caring for the dying? It is not only when we travel to the remote areas of the world that we can win souls for the Lord.

105

There are souls in need of your love and support—in your home/family, neighborhood, church, work, school or wherever you may be. It may be someone in Walmart (or some other store) struggling to get enough money to buy food or something very essential for his/her family, while you are there to buy what you want, not necessarily your need. Are you willing to spare that money for your wants for someone's needs? You can be a blessing in a big or small way. The most important thing is to be ready and willing when met with such situations. I pray that God will grant us all the grace to "Brighten the corner, wherever we are," in the mighty name of Jesus. Amen!

Song of Meditation "Brighten the Corner Where You Are"
By Ina D. Ogdon (1913)

1. Do not wait until some deed of greatness you may do,

Do not wait to shed your light afar;

To the many duties ever near you now be true,

Brighten the corner where you are.

Refrain

Brighten the corner where you are!

Brighten the corner where you are!

Someone far from harbor you may guide across the bar;

Brighten the corner where you are!

2. Just above are clouded skies that you may help to clear,

Let not narrow self your way debar;

Though into one heart alone may fall your song of cheer,

Brighten the corner where you are.

3. Here for all your talent you may surely find a need,

Here reflect the bright and Morning Star;

Even from your humble hand the Bread of Life may feed,

Brighten the corner where you are.

YOU HAVE BEEN CALLED

Are you feeling inadequate or unqualified for the task God has called you to do? Remember, "He did not call the qualified, but He has promised to qualify the ones He has called," just as He did for Moses, who had impaired speech issues. What is my own issue, and what is yours that the Lord is not capable of "fixing?" Darling child of God, right there where you are reading this book, take the time to give your weakness/es or issue/s to God in prayer. Hand ALL your "issues" over to Him and allow Him to bring the best out of you, for His Glory, in the name of Jesus. I pray that through you, souls will be drawn to God; loneliness, anxiety or depression will not have power over you or any member of your family, church family, coworkers, patients and ANYONE God will place in your path. As a leader, the ones under you will not be running around for safety or thinking they need a gun, just to protect themselves. May ALL lives matter whenever and wherever you lead, in the name of Jesus. May God use you as a leader to eradicate racism, injustice, discrimination and superiority/inferiority complexes. As a leader, may God grant you the grace to seek the souls that are sore and very weak. May he help you bring the wanderers, weary and the hopeless people back to Him. May you rule/lead through the guidance of God/Holy Spirit. May the love of God reign in all our hearts, in the mighty name of Jesus. Amen!

Song of Meditation "Seeking the Lost" By William A. Ogden

1. Seeking the lost-yes, kindly entreating
Wanderers on the mountain astray
"Come unto Me," His message repeating,
Words of the Master speaking today.

Refrain
Ladies: (Going afar) (Upon the mountain)
Men: Going afar Upon the mountain
Ladies: (Bringing the wand'rer back again,) back again
Men: Bringing the wand'rer back again, back again
Ladies: Into the fold of my Redeemer,
Men: Into the fold of my Redeemer
Ladies: (Jesus, the Lamb +for sinners slain,) for sinners slain
Men: Jesus, the lamb +for sinners slain, for sinners slain

2. Seeking the lost-and pointing to Jesus
Souls that are weak and hearts that are sore,
Leading them forth in ways of salvation,
Showing the path to life evermore.

3. Thus, I would go on missions of mercy
Following Christ from day unto day,
Cheering the faint and raising the fallen,
Pointing the lost to Jesus, the Way

STAND UP FOR THE RIGHT

We should be able to "call a spade a spade" with the guidance of the Holy Spirit. We must not be intimidated or afraid of standing up for the right and fighting for the oppressed. It was the wisdom God gave to Solomon that helped him resolve the challenging case brought to him. He said with all authority, "Give the first woman the living child, and by no means kill him; she is his mother" (He was very certain that the woman was the mother of the living child). He did not depend on his own understanding. He prayed for wisdom. You can imagine if he were to be confused as many of our leaders are today. Or imagine if he focused on which of the women had the highest education/degree, position or fame.

Just picture the scenario. If King Solomon had brought himself so low by having an affair with one of these women, or if he was gaining something from the friendship and did not want to mess the relationship up, he wouldn't have been able to judge right, most especially if the second woman who wanted the child killed, was his mistress or "beneficiary," he could have killed the poor baby as suggested by the woman to maintain the "friendship." With God's help, he made the right judgment, and all Israel heard of it, and they feared the king, for they saw that the wisdom of God was in him to administer justice. I pray that the world will see God's wisdom in us, in the way we handle things, in the mighty name of Jesus. Amen!

How many people have turned to drugs, alcohol or other bad influences? How many are in jail? Some are in psychiatric hospitals because they had to learn how to wear the "veil/makeup" to avoid being judged, ridiculed or facing unnecessary embarrassments. How many did not get the help they needed when it was needed most, and they decided to kill themselves? I pray we will be willing to give of our time, ears and all that we need to give off to the Master and be there for one another, in the name of Jesus. We are to be determined to help someone or encourage ourselves that suicide is **NOT** the solution to any form of challenges we may be facing. Remember, there is a light at the end of the tunnel, so don't give up. All of us are soldiers of the cross. Let us stand up for Jesus! Despite the challenges and trials, let us stand up for the right. Things may be very rough now, but our God is alive and FAITHFUL! Our roses will bloom again, in the name of Jesus. Amen!

Song of Meditation "Stand Up, Stand Up for Jesus!" By
George Duffield Jr. (1858)

1. Stand up! Stand up for Jesus!
Ye soldiers of the cross;
Lift high His royal banner,
It must not suffer loss:
From vict'ry unto vict'ry
His army shall He lead,

Till every foe is vanquished
And Christ is Lord indeed.

2. Stand up! Stand up for Jesus!
The trumpet call obey;
Forth to the mighty conflict
In this His glorious day.
Ye that are men, now serve Him
Against unnumbered foes;
Let courage rise with danger.
And strength to strength oppose.

3. Stand up! Stand up for Jesus!
Stand in His strength alone;
The arm of flesh will fail you;
Ye dare not trust your own.
Put on the Gospel armor,
And, watching unto prayer,
Where duty calls, or danger,
Be never wanting there.

4. Stand up! Stand up for Jesus!
The strife will not be long:
This day the noise of battle,
The next the victor's song;
To him that overcometh
A crown of life shall be;
He, with the King of glory,
Shall reign eternally.

CRYING IN THE "RAIN"

The smiling faces we see at work, churches, schools or everywhere may not be real. There may be tears/sorrow under the "makeup/veil." If you happen to have the opportunity to know what others are going through, you will be amazed and may find it difficult to believe. Many times, these people put their "issues" aside to be vessels of encouragement to others. You may be wondering: What is she talking about? How can one be smiling and be having issues at the same time? When did he/she go through the heartaches of life? He/she was ALWAYS smiling, ALWAYS available to lend listening ears and ALWAYS ready to praise the Lord. I am very sorry to inform you that people may be the opposite of what you see outside. The smile you have been seeing may not be there always, just that they might have learned to do their "crying" in the "rain," It has been said: "The prettiest eyes have cried the most tears."

Be reminded that everyone you meet has "issues." Be gentle, loving, caring and compassionate. If all the above mentioned are not possible for you to do, just see to it that you DO NOT add to the "load" others are carrying: "Loads" of rejection, loneliness, joblessness, abuses of different types, injustice, discrimination and other "loads" they may be carrying that is weighing them down. I tell you: they could be very heavy. I pray that God will snatch any form of "load" that is making you feel anxious, depressed, unwanted or giving you any form of negative feeling, in the mighty name of Jesus. Amen!

Song of Meditation "Try a Little Kindness" By Glen Campbell (1970)

You may be crying for reasons only known to you and your Lord for now. Count it ALL joy darling brother/sister. Have faith in God. Your faith in Him will produce patience. God will use your trials to shape you. By His grace, you will NOT lack ANYTHING, in the mighty name of Jesus. Amen!

Bible Verses for Encouragements

It is written: *"My brethren, count it all joy when you fall into various trials, knowing that the testing of your faith produces patience. But let patience have its perfect work, that you may be perfect and complete, lacking nothing"* (James 1:2-4 NKJV).

"And not only that, but we also glory in tribulations, knowing that tribulation produces perseverance; and perseverance, character; and character, hope" (Romans 5:3-4 NKJV).

"In this you greatly rejoice, though now for a little while, if need be, you have been grieved by various trials, that the genuineness of your faith, being much more precious than gold that perishes,

114

though it is tested by fire, may be found to praise, honor, and glory at the revelation of Jesus Christ (1 Peter 1:6-7 NKJV).

"God is our refuge and strength, A very present help in trouble. Therefore, we will not fear, even though the earth be removed, and though the mountains be carried into the midst of the sea; Though its waters roar and be troubled, though the mountains shake with its swelling. Selah" (Psalm 46:1-3 NKJV).

"Then he said to them, "Go your way, eat the fat, drink the sweet, and send portions to those for whom nothing is prepared; for this day is holy to our Lord. Do not sorrow, for the joy of the LORD is your strength" (Nehemiah 8:10 NKJV).

"The LORD is my light and my salvation; Whom shall, I fear? The LORD is the strength of my life; Of whom shall I be afraid? When the wicked came against me to eat up my flesh, my enemies and foes, they stumbled and fell. Though an army may encamp against me, my heart shall not fear; Though war may rise against me, in this I will be confident" (Psalm 27:1-3 NKJV).

"Have I not commanded you? Be strong and of good courage; do not be afraid, nor be dismayed, for the LORD your God is with you wherever you go" (Joshua 1:9 NKJV).

"The LORD is near to all who call upon Him, to all who call upon Him in truth. He will fulfill the desire of those who fear Him; He also will hear their cry and save them" (Psalm 145:18-19 NKJV).

It is okay to cry! *To everything there is a season, a time for every purpose under heaven: And a time to build up; A time to weep, and a time to laugh; A time to mourn, and a time to dance"* (Ecclesiastes 3:1 & 4 NKJV). The world we live in has its ups and downs. It's like a roller-coaster. The Lord did not promise that we will only see sunshine, but He promised that He will be with us every step of the way. It is written: *"These things I have spoken to you, that in Me you may have peace. In the world you will have tribulation; but be of good cheer, I have overcome the world"* (John 16:33 NKJV). The Bible says: *"Yet man is born to trouble, as the sparks fly upward"* (Job 5:7 NKJV). The Lord wants us to be *"Rejoicing in hope, patient in tribulation, continuing steadfastly in prayer"* (Romans 12:12 NKJV). May He continue to be our guide in this "wilderness journey." He is our rock of ages. May He make us ALL that He wants us to be for him, as we helplessly look up to Him for grace. May we continue to hide ourselves in Him, and allow Him to wipe our tears away, in the mighty name of Jesus. Amen!

Song of Meditation "Rock of Ages, Cleft for Me" By Augustus Toplady (1776)

1. Rock of Ages, cleft for me,
Let me hide myself in Thee;
Let the water and the blood,
From Thy riven side which flowed,
Be of sin the double cure,
Save me from its guilt and power.

116

2. Not the labor of my hands
Can fulfill Thy law's demands;
Could my zeal no respite know,
Could my tears forever flow,
All could never sin erase,
Thou must save, and save by grace.

3. Nothing in my hands I bring,
Simply to Thy cross I cling;
Naked, come to Thee for dress,
Helpless, look to Thee for grace:
Foul, I to the fountain fly,
Wash me, Savior, or I die.

4. While I draw this fleeting breath,
When mine eyes shall close in death,
When I soar to worlds unknown,
See Thee on Thy judgment throne,
Rock of Ages, cleft for me,
Let me hide myself in Thee

Our society sees crying or expression of emotions as signs of weakness. You might have heard the saying "Big girls don't cry," and in the "standard" of the world men/boys are not supposed to cry at all. **IT IS A LIE.** There is a record in the Bible that *"Jesus wept"* (John 11:35 NKJV). Can any man be more "real" than He is? It is ALL RIGHT for "real" boys, men, ladies, pastors or anyone to cry or express their emotions. Brethren, **IT IS OKAY**

TO CRY! Let it out if you must. You will be relieved of the pent-up emotions, which will prevent UNNECESSARY "explosion." Crying is not a sign of weakness, please! It just shows that you have feelings and that you are **"REAL."** I pray that God will wipe your tears away and put an end to WHATEVER is making you cry, in the mighty name of Jesus. Amen! It is written: *"And God will wipe away every tear from their eyes; there shall be no more death, nor sorrow, nor crying. There shall be no more pain, for the former things have passed away"* (Revelation 21:4 NKJV).

It is written: *"Then He who sat on the throne said, "Behold, I make all things new." And He said to me, "Write, for these words are true and faithful." And He said to me, "It is done! I am the Alpha and the Omega, the beginning and the end. I will give of the fountain of the water of life freely to him who thirsts"* (Revelation 21:5-6 NKJV). Be reminded, *"God's anger is but for a moment, His favor is for life; Weeping may endure for a night, but joy comes in the morning"* (Psalm 30:5). Morning is coming, dear child of God. Keep on holding on because, soon and very soon, we are going to see our Father. There will be no more crying, no more sorrow, no dying, no heartache or anything that will get us down, in the mighty name of Jesus. Amen. DO NOT GIVE UP, PLEASE!

118

Song of Meditation "Sing the Wondrous Love of Jesus" E. E. Hewitt (1898)

1. Sing the wondrous love of Jesus,
   Sing His mercy and His grace;
   In the mansions bright and blessed
   He'll prepare for us a place.

Refrain:
When we all get to heaven,
what a day of rejoicing that will be!
When we all see Jesus,
we'll sing and shout the victory!

2. While we walk the pilgrim pathway
   Clouds will overspread the sky;
   But when trav'ling days are over
   Not a shadow, not a sigh.

3. Let us then be true and faithful,
   Trusting, serving ev'ry day;
   Just one glimpse of Him in glory
   Will the toils of life repay.

4. Onward to the prize before us!
   Soon His beauty we'll behold;
   Soon the pearly gates will open–
   We shall tread the streets of gold.

YOUR TEARS MOVE GOD

You might have had a very bad experience with the ones you have shared your concerns with, and this might have affected your trust level adversely. It is written: *"Behold, the LORD's hand is not shortened, that it cannot save; Nor His ear heavy, that it cannot hear"* (Isaiah 59:1 NKJV). God listens through your heart. He sees and knows all that is happening in your life. Things you are ashamed/afraid to talk about, He knows. He hears your "midnight cries"; he sees the crying in the "rain" and how you cry yourself to sleep. God feels your pain, and He is not judging you. He loves you. So, fear not; He is able to save you and He will, in the name of Jesus. Let it be known that your tears are stored up in God's "bottle." It is written, *"You number my wanderings; Put my tears into Your bottle; Are they not in Your book"* (Psalm 56:8 NKJV). By the grace of God, you have cried your last cry yesterday. The joy of the Lord is your strength. May He put an end to your crying and fill your mouth with laughter, in the mighty name of Jesus. Amen!

Song of Meditation "The Joy of The Lord, Is My Strength"
By Unknown Artiste

Chorus

The joy of the Lord, is my strength

The joy of the Lord, is my strength

The joy of the Lord, is my strength

The joy of the Lord, is my strength

1. He heals the broken-hearted, and they cry no more

He heals the broken-hearted, and they cry no more

He heals the broken-hearted, and they cry no more

The joy of the LORD is my strength!

2. He gives me living water, and I thirst no more

He gives me living water, and I thirst no more

He gives me living water, and I thirst no more

The joy of the LORD is my strength!

3. He fills my mouth with laughter

Ha, ha, ha, ha, ha

He fills my mouth with laughter

Ha, ha, ha, ha, ha

He fills my mouth with laughter

Ha, ha, ha, ha, ha

The joy of the LORD is my strength!

Have you been provoked to cry? The story of Hannah and Peninnah shows how God is moved when we cry unto Him. It is written: *"And her rival also provoked her severely, to make her miserable, because the LORD had closed her womb. So, it was, year by year, when she went up to the house of the LORD, that she provoked her; therefore, she **WEPT** and did not eat"* (1 Samuel 1:6-8 NKJV; emphasis added).

I love the New International Reader's version: *"Peninnah teased Hannah to make her angry. She did it because the LORD had kept Hannah from having children. Peninnah teased Hannah year after year. Every time Hannah would go up to the house of the LORD, Elkanah's other wife would tease her. She would keep doing it **until Hannah cried and wouldn't eat.** Her husband Elkanah would say to her, "Hannah, why are you crying? Why don't you eat? Why are you so unhappy? Don't I mean more to you than ten sons"* (1 Samuel 1:6-8 NIV, emphasis added)

What is it that you are crying to God for? I don't know how long you have been crying. You may be so provoked now and don't know what to do. I am letting you know that the same God who answered Hannah's prayer is alive. He is able and willing to answer your own prayers too, according to His will, in the name of Jesus. Let it be known that your tears move God. By His grace, I pray that your "Peninnahs" will soon come and rejoice with you, in the name of Jesus. Your "Samuel" is coming, and Jesus Himself will be your "Elkanah," supporting and encouraging you ALL through the way until "Samuel" arrives, in the mighty name of

Jesus. (The "Samuel" here refers to your joy, victory, deliverance or ANYTHING you have been waiting on God for, in the name of Jesus). Take time to talk to Him, claim His promises and believe that He has answered you. So, shall it be for you, in the name of Jesus. Amen! It is written: *"The eyes of the LORD are on the righteous, and His ears are open to their cry"* (Psalm 34:15 NKJV). May the good Lord answer our prayers, in the mighty name of Jesus. Amen!

DEPRESSION IS REAL

With all that is going on in the world today, we would all agree that we have experienced some form of down moments, one way or another. The way we handle things may be what is different. Some may turn to alcohol, drugs, promiscuity, gambling, smoking or whatever may distract them from the issue or bring some form of relief, even if it is temporary. Unfortunately, poor decisions may result in complicated situations later in life. For instance, one may become a drug addict through the use of drugs; alcohol consumption may make one become an alcoholic, which may also result in some forms of medical problems; promiscuity may lead to sexually transmitted infections and other things.

When one is feeling down, it is not unusual to want to withdraw into one's "shell," hide and try to cover up the "wounds." Darling child of God, I want to tell you that depression is real, but our God is FAITHFUL! If you are feeling down, and you notice that it is getting out of hand, kindly seek help. If you have been prescribed medication to help with the depression, kindly take it as prescribed; do not stop abruptly because it may result in unpleasant side effects. Talk to your doctor/provider if you have any questions, please. May the Lord restore your joy and take the depression away, in the mighty name of Jesus. Amen! Let it be known to you that Jesus understands what you are going through.

Don't worry about the "stigma"; we all have issues, and God is not done working with ANY of us. Don't let ANYONE make you feel like they are better than you. We are all going through "remodeling." The year 2020 affected the whole world, one way or another, and we are under "construction." If we let go and let God take total control of our lives, He will calm our anxious hearts and teach us how to take life one day at a time. May the good Lord grant us the serenity to accept the things we cannot change, and may He continue to guide and protect us all, in the mighty name of Jesus. Amen!

Prayer

Heavenly Father, we have acknowledged that depression is real, but You are faithful! May we be open and willing to get help from You and the helpers You will send to us, in the name of Jesus. May we acknowledge Your love, presence, faithfulness, protection, grace and mercy in our lives. Forgive us of the pretense and the way we might have misrepresented You. Turn things around for good, Lord. We reject the spirit of anxiety, depression, suicide/homicide ideations, in the mighty name of Jesus. Amen!

I don't know the challenges you are facing, but just a quick reminder that it will not last, in the name of Jesus. REMEMBER! Jesus went from the cross to the grave, from the grave to the sky. HALLELUJAH! He was victorious. Your roses will bloom again, and you will be victorious in the end, by the special grace of God.

I want to stress that when Jesus was passing through His trying periods, He consulted His heavenly Father and asked His disciples to pray with Him. He did not keep it to Himself. It is very important that we seek help as needed. The rate at which things are happening in the world today and the effects these things are having on all of us are of great concern. I have seen enough to know and admit that ANYONE can "trip" and "fall" into the "valley" of depression/suicide. I pray that God will continue to guide and uphold us with His right hand of righteousness, in the name of Jesus. Amen!

Depression is not diagnosed by blood tests or imaging studies. This makes it different from other medical conditions that can be easily diagnosed. The health providers base their diagnoses on the history given by patients. This depends on whether the patient is telling the truth or not. It is important that you tell your stories and be truthful about them to the ones who will help you. I pray that God will direct you to the right people at the right time, in the name of Jesus. Amen! Diagnosing one with depression or suicidal ideation can be very challenging due to the "makeup," "powders/concealers," "nice perfume," "hair color dyes," fine cloths and other things people use to cover up. The care providers may not know that one is depressed or planning to "help" God put an end to the sufferings. GOOD NEWS! The OMNISCIENT God knows it ALL. HALLELUJAH! Run to His "emergency room" today. Tell Him all about your concerns, worries and trials. It is time to receive your healing. Do not worry about the "bill." Jesus

126

has paid it all with His precious blood on the cross of Calvary. He paid EVERYTHING in FULL. Hallelujah!

Song of Meditation "I Must Tell Jesus" By Elisha A. Hoffman (1894)

1. I must tell Jesus all of my trials,
I cannot bear these burdens alone;
In my distress, He kindly will help me,
He ever loves and cares for His own.

Refrain:
I must tell Jesus! I must tell Jesus!
I cannot bear my burdens alone;
I must tell Jesus! I must tell Jesus!
Jesus can help me, Jesus alone.

2. I must tell Jesus all of my troubles,
He is a kind, compassionate Friend;
If I but ask Him He will deliver,
Make of my troubles quickly an end.

3. Tempted and tried I need a great Savior,
One who can help my burdens to bear;
I must tell Jesus, I must tell Jesus:
He all my cares and sorrows will share.

4. What must I do when worldliness calls me?
What must I do when tempted to sin?
I must tell Jesus, and He will help me
Over the world the vict'ry to win.

Nobody can speak for you. You know yourself and the level of your stress, anxiety or discouragement. You know how low your "tank" is. May God grant you the grace to know where and when to fill it up. May the Lord fill your cup for you, in the name of Jesus. Amen! I will say it again: Kindly seek the appropriate help. Don't keep things to yourself, please! Kindly talk to people that you trust. Those who can help you. People who will go to the "garden" with you, even if they will fall asleep there like the disciples did in the garden of Gethsemane when they went with Jesus. It is written: *"Then He came and found them sleeping, and said to Peter, "Simon, are you sleeping? Could you not watch one hour?"* (Mark 14:37 NKJV). It is better to have sincere and faithful friends who will go to the "garden" with you and sleep than to have the ones who will be wide awake only to gossip, mock, distract, stress or gang up against you. Their flesh may be weak, but their spirit is willing.

Moreover, the Lord said He will not share His glory with anyone. So, it is even better for your friends to sleep in the "garden" so that they don't wake up one day and claim the glory that does not belong to them. Jesus has promised that He will be with you during your trying times. Darling child of God, it is very important to know that you are **NEVER ALONE!** It is written: *"Teaching them to observe all things that I have commanded you; and lo, I am with you always, even to the end of the age"* (Matthew 28:2 NKJV). The Lord is with you. God is a promise keeper. **HE**

WILL NEVER FAIL. Glory hallelujah! He sent an angel to Jesus during His trying period. It is written: *"Then an angel appeared to Him from heaven, strengthening Him"* (Luke 22:43 NKJV). I pray that during your challenging periods, you will feel the presence of God and the host of heaven walking and talking to you. May they comfort, encourage and strengthen you. I pray that you will hear His sweet and tender voice telling you that you are His own, in the name of Jesus. Amen!

Song of Meditation "I Come to the Garden Alone" By Austin Miles (1913)

1. I come to the garden alone
While the dew is still on the roses
And the voice I hear falling on my ear
The Son of God discloses.

Refrain:
And He walks with me, and He talks with me,
And He tells me I am His own;
And the joy we share as we tarry there,
None other has ever known.

2. He speaks, and the sound of His voice,
Is so sweet the birds hush their singing,
And the melody that He gave to me
Within my heart is ringing.

3. I'd stay in the garden with Him
Though the night around me be falling,
But He bids me go; through the voice of woe
His voice to me is calling.

129

BE ANXIOUS FOR NOTHING

D arling child of God, with God on your side, you are NEVER alone. He walks and talks with you, telling you that you belong to Him. This is an AMAZING and assuring antidepressant!

Despite all the various things happening in the world today that can make one feel very insecure, anxious and depressed, to the point that one may even want to throw in the towel and die, killings here and there, weather disasters and other challenging things we have to deal with are robbing us of living fulfilled lives, stealing our joys and possessions. Moreover, racism (that I call "autoimmune disease") is destroying America and other parts of the world along with their tribal problems, religious conflicts, not to mention job insecurity, marital problems, wars and rumors of war. Rebellious children, men running to and fro for greener pastures, leaving families and loved ones with the hope of returning home to their families, only to end up in the hands of the cruel ones—many have lost their lives in the process. It is very sad! May God help us to cast our cares upon Him, drop our burdens at His feet and NEVER go back to them.

It is true that we don't know what tomorrow holds, and we don't even know what to do. It is written: "*Be anxious for nothing, but in everything by prayer and supplication, with thanksgiving, let your requests be made known to God; and the peace of God, which surpasses all understanding, will guard your hearts and minds through Christ Jesus"* (Philippians 4:6-8 NKJV). This is God's message to you: *"Say to those who are fearful-hearted, 'Be strong, do not fear! Behold, your God will come with vengeance, with the recompense of God; He will come and save you'"* (Isaiah 35:4 NKJV). *"Let not your heart be troubled; you believe in God, believe also in Me"* (John 14:1 NKJV). It is written: *"And which of you by worrying can add one cubit to his stature? If you then are not able to do the least, why are you anxious for the rest? Consider the lilies, how they grow: they neither toil nor spin; and yet I say to you, even Solomon in all his glory was not arrayed like one of these. If then God so clothes the grass, which today is in the field and tomorrow is thrown into the oven, how much more will He clothe you, O you of little faith? "And do not seek what you should eat or what you should drink, nor have an anxious mind. For all these things the nations of the world seek after, and your Father knows that you need these things. But seek the kingdom of God, and all these things shall be added to you"* (Luke 12:25-31 NKJV). *"Therefore, do not worry about tomorrow, for tomorrow will worry about its own things. Sufficient for the day is its own trouble"* (Matthew 6:34 NKJV). May the spirit of God overshadow the spirit of fear and restore your confidence, trust, faith, hope and all you need to live a fulfilled life, in the mighty name of Jesus. Amen!

Song of Meditation "Come, Every Soul by Sin Oppressed"

By John H. Stockton (1874)

1. Come, every soul by sin oppressed,

   there's mercy with the Lord,

   and He will surely give you rest

   by trusting in His word.

   Refrain

   Only trust Him, only trust Him,

   only trust Him now;

   He will save you, He will save you.

   He will save you now.

2. For Jesus shed His precious blood

   rich blessings to bestow;

   plunge now into the crimson flood

   that washes white as snow.

3. Yes, Jesus is the truth, the way,

   that leads you into rest;

   believe in Him without delay,

   and you are fully blest.

4. Come, then, and join this holy band,

   and on to glory go,

   to dwell in that celestial land

   where joys immortal flow.

WAS JESUS DEPRESSED, ANXIOUS OR SUICIDAL?

NO, NOT AT ALL! Darling brother/sister in the Lord, I just want to reinforce that it is ALL RIGHT to cry, feel sad or sorrowful during sad moments—for instance, when a loved one dies or when we have a challenging situation that makes us emotional or something challenges our happiness. If you notice that the crying or sadness is becoming an everyday affair, I highly recommend that we seek help from your church pastor, friends, family, counselor/therapist or psychiatrist, depending on the severity of your sorrow/sadness, pain, worries or depression. It may help to know that Jesus passed through what you and I passed/are passing through. It was not ALL rosy for Him when he was here on earth. The difference is that He did not sin. He was referred to as a "man of sorrow." It is written: *"He is despised and rejected by men. A Man of sorrows and acquainted with grief. And we hid, as it were, our faces from Him; He was despised, and we did not esteem Him. Surely, He has borne our griefs and carried our sorrows; yet we esteemed Him stricken, smitten by God, and afflicted. But He was wounded for our transgressions, He was bruised for our iniquities; the chastisement for our peace was upon Him, and by His stripes we are healed"* (Isaiah 53:3-5 NKJV). HALLELUJAH!

Certain challenges in life are inevitable. Some of these challenges could be so painful, scary and very devastating that one may feel the whole world is collapsing all around. Jesus felt this agony. It is written: *"And being in agony, He prayed more earnestly. Then His sweat became like great drops of blood falling down to the ground"* (Luke 22:44 NKJV). The medical term for this is: "HEMATIDROSIS." If Jesus were to be here today, the psychiatrist would have tried to diagnose Him as depressed and suicidal, as evidenced by His statement, *"My soul is exceedingly sorrowful, **even to death**"* (Mark 14:34; emphasis added). Our sorrows, pain, rejections and griefs are nowhere comparable to what Jesus went through for our redemption. Despite His agony, depression, anxiety, suicidal/homicide ideations, all failed. They couldn't get to Him or get Him down. It was possible for Him to do something simple as commanding the ones nailing Him to the cross to die, but He did not. He was focused. It is written: *"He was oppressed and He was afflicted, yet He opened not His mouth; He was led as a lamb to the slaughter, and as a sheep before its shearers is silent, So He opened not His mouth"* (Isaiah 53:7 NKJV). He knew He had to die for us to be saved, so He surrendered Himself to be killed. May God keep us focused and prevent all that is happening around us from distracting us, in the name of Jesus.

During this very challenging point in the life of Jesus, He reached out to His disciples for support. He did not isolate Himself. He expressed His feelings, AS NEEDED and was very careful about the ways He went about this. He went into the garden of Gethsemane with His disciples to pray. It is written: *"Then they came to a place which was named Gethsemane; and He said to His disciples, "Sit here while I pray." And He took Peter, James, and John with Him, and He began to be troubled and deeply distressed. Then He said to them, "My soul is exceedingly sorrowful, even to death. Stay here and watch." He went a little farther, and fell on the ground, and prayed that if it were possible, the hour might pass from Him. And He said, "Abba, Father, all things are possible for You. Take this cup away from Me; nevertheless, not what I will, but what You will"* (Mark 14:32-36 NKJV). MERCY!

When we are going through our "challenging" moments, do we still acknowledge God, or are we basing our feelings on "flesh" or our heart's desires? Do we take time to consult with God for ONLY His will be done? Some of us depend on the approval of others so much that the fear of rejection or what people will say may make us do what we are not supposed to do. It is written: *"What then shall we say to these things? If God is for us, who can be against us? He who did not spare His own Son, but delivered Him up for us all, how shall He not with Him also freely give us all things? Who shall bring a charge against God's elect? It is God who justifies. Who is he who condemns? It is Christ who died, and furthermore is also risen, who is even at the right hand of God, who also makes intercession for us. Who shall separate us from the love of Christ? Shall tribulation, or distress, or persecution, or famine, or nakedness, or peril, or sword?"* (Romans 8:31-35 NKJV). Depression, grief/sorrow or things we call behavioral health issues will not overpower us. As small and weak as our strength may be, the Lord is our EVERYTHING. He has paid it ALL. We are complete in Him. Hallelujah, Amen!

Song of Meditation "Jesus Paid it All" By Elvina M. Hall.
(1865)

1. I hear the Savior say,
"Thy strength indeed is small;
Child of weakness, watch and pray,
Find in Me thine all in all."

Refrain
Jesus paid it all,
All to Him I owe;
Sin had left a crimson stain,
He washed it white as snow.

2. For nothing good have I
Whereby Thy grace to claim;
I'll wash my garments white
In the blood of Calv'ry's Lamb.

3. And now complete in Him,
My robe, His righteousness,
Close sheltered 'neath His side,
I am divinely blest.

4. Lord, now indeed I find
Thy pow'r, and Thine alone,
Can change the leper's spots
And melt the heart of stone.

5. When from my dying bed
My ransomed soul shall rise,
"Jesus died my soul to save,"
Shall rend the vaulted skies.

6. And when before the throne
I stand in Him complete,
I'll lay my trophies down,
All down at Jesus' feet.

Talk about sorrow and excruciating pain; Jesus experienced it. He went through all the agony for us to be saved. He was wounded for our transgressions. Killing ourselves or someone else is a way of showing Him that He only came to waste His time and His precious blood by dying on the cross. We are indirectly nailing Him to the cross daily through the ways we live, the ways we deal with others and our sinful nature. No matter our challenges, suicide/homicide is NEVER the solution, please. In case we have forgotten all that Jesus had to go through for us, I will recommend that we watch the movie "Passion of Christ" again or read Matthew 27, Mark 15, Luke 23 and John 19.

It is written, *"But He was wounded for our transgressions, He was bruised for our iniquities; The chastisement for our peace was upon Him, and by His stripes we are healed. All we like sheep have gone astray; We have turned, everyone, to his own way; and the LORD has laid on Him the iniquity of us all. He was oppressed and He was afflicted, yet He opened not His mouth; He was led as a lamb to the slaughter, and as a sheep before its shearers is silent, so He opened not His mouth. He was taken from prison and from judgment, and who will declare His generation? For He was cut off from the land of the living; For the transgressions of My people, He was stricken"* (Isaiah 53:5-8 NKJV). May His sufferings on the cross, for you and me, NEVER be in vain, in the mighty name of Jesus. Amen!

Song of Meditation "Man of Sorrows, What A Name" By Philip P. Bliss (1875)

1 Man of sorrows what a name
for the Son of God, who came
ruined sinners to reclaim:
Hallelujah, what a Savior!

2 Bearing shame and scoffing rude,
in my place condemned he stood,
sealed my pardon with his blood:
Hallelujah, what a Savior!

3 Guilty, helpless, lost were we;
blameless Lamb of God was he,
sacrificed to set us free:
Hallelujah, what a Savior!

4 He was lifted up to die;
"It is finished" was his cry;
now in heaven exalted high:
Hallelujah, what a Savior!

5 When he comes, our glorious King,
all his ransomed home to bring,
then anew this song we'll sing:
Hallelujah, what a Savior!

DO NOT GIVE UP!

We live in a very crazy and troublesome world. Family members dying, COVID-19 claiming lives, preventing churches and other gatherings from coming together, people losing their jobs, single parenthood, abuses of different kinds, racism, injustice, and many other reasons out there could lead to severe anxiety, depression and other behavioral issues, as mentioned earlier. Darling child of God, we know that challenges may come, but we are to keep reminding ourselves that our Savior is ALWAYS with us. He promised NEVER to tempt us more than what we can handle. It is written: *"No temptation has overtaken you except such as is common to man; but God is faithful, who will not allow you to be tempted beyond what you are able, but with the temptation will also make the way of escape, that you may be able to bear it"* (1 Corinthians 10:13 NKJV). May God grant us the grace to hold on to the end and keep trusting in Him, in the name of Jesus. Amen!

These Bible verses are some of the reasons we cannot afford to give up. We must remind ourselves that we are loved by the One who matters most. He will NEVER give up on us. It is written: *"See, I have inscribed you on the palms of My hands; Your walls are continually before Me"* (Isaiah 49:16 NKJV). It is written: *"But God demonstrates His own love toward us, in that while we were still sinners, Christ died for us"* (Romans 5:8 NKJV).

Furthermore, the Bible says: *"Behold what manner of love the Father has bestowed on us, that we should be called children of God! Therefore, the world does not know us, because it did not know Him"* (1 John 3:1 NKJV). You are very precious in the sight of God. Even when we have given up on ourselves, He still loves and cares for us. He is the God who stays. He does not see us the way we see ourselves, and the impression of the world does not matter to Him. He will FOREVER be by our sides, through thin and thick, rain or sunshine. He will NEVER leave us alone to face our challenges by ourselves, in the mighty name of Jesus. DON'T GIVE UP, PLEASE!

Song of Meditation "The God Who Stays" By Matthew West (2019)

Song of Meditation "Jesus Loves Me, This I Know" By Anna Bartlett Warner (1859)

1. Jesus loves me, this I know,
   for the Bible tells me so.
   Little ones to him belong;
   they are weak, but he is strong.

Refrain:
Yes, Jesus loves me! Yes, Jesus loves me!
Yes, Jesus loves me! The Bible tells me so.

2. Jesus loves me he who died
heaven's gate to open wide.
He will wash away my sin,
let his little child come in.

3. Jesus loves me, this I know,
as he loved so long ago,
taking children on his knee,
saying, "Let them come to me."

FEAR NOT

The world is filled with anxiety/fear of the unknown. People are desperately looking for solutions. We have been encouraging ourselves to hold on to God and trust Him to see us through. I just want to quickly remind you that God does not operate on our level. It is written:

"For My thoughts are not your thoughts, nor are your ways My ways," says the LORD. "For as the heavens are higher than the earth, so are My ways higher than your ways and My thoughts than your thoughts" (Isaiah 55:8-9 NKJV).

We may not really understand some of the things God does, and we may question WHY? You have to understand, "To have God in your life, doesn't mean sailing on a boat with no storms, it simply means: Having a boat that no storm can sink" (author unknown). Moreover, we are to realize, "Having God in your boat doesn't mean that you will not face any storm. It means that no storm can sink your boat! Walk in faith, and you will never walk alone" (author unknown). May God help us and take away the fear of the unknown; may we not forget that He has promised to take care of us. May we remain under His wings of love and protection, in the name of Jesus. I pray that God will calm your storms, grant you peace, renew your strength and help you smile/laugh again, in the mighty name of Jesus. Amen!

Song of Meditation "God Will Take Care of You" By Civilla D. Martin (1904)

1. Be not dismayed whate'er betide,
God will take care of you;
Beneath His wings of love abide,
God will take care of you.

Refrain
God will take care of you,
Through every day, o'er all the way;
He will take care of you,
God will take care of you.

2. Through days of toil when heart doth fail,
God will take care of you;
When dangers fierce your path assail,
God will take care of you.

3. All you may need He will provide,
God will take care of you;
Nothing you ask will be denied,
God will take care of you.

4. No matter what may be the test,
God will take care of you;
Lean, weary one, upon His breast,
God will take care of you.

144

Bible Verses for The Soul

"These things I have spoken to you, that in Me you may have peace. In the world you will have tribulation; but be of good cheer, I have overcome the world" (John 16:33 NKJV).

"Fear not, for I am with you; Be not dismayed, for I am your God. I will strengthen you, Yes, I will help you, I will uphold you with My righteous right hand" (Isaiah 41:10 NKJV).

"But even if you should suffer for righteousness' sake, you are blessed. "And do not be afraid of their threats, nor be troubled" (1 Peter 3:14 NKJV).

"But those who wait on the LORD shall renew their strength; They shall mount up with wings like eagles, they shall run and not be weary, they shall walk and not faint"
(Isaiah 40:31 NKJV).

"Say to those who are fearful-hearted, 'Be strong, do not fear! Behold, your God will come with vengeance, With the recompense of God; He will come and save you'" (Isaiah 35:4 NKJV).

Song of Meditation "Peace, Perfect Peace" By Edward Henry Bickersteth

1. Peace, perfect peace, in this dark world of sin?
The blood of Jesus whispers peace within.

2. Peace, perfect peace, by thronging duties pressed?
To do the will of Jesus, this is rest.

3. Peace, perfect peace, with sorrows surging round?
On Jesus' bosom naught but calm is found.

4. Peace, perfect peace, 'mid suffering's sharpest throes?
The sympathy of Jesus breathes repose.

5. Peace, perfect peace, with loved ones far away?
In Jesus' keeping we are safe, and they.

6. Peace, perfect peace, our future all unknown?
Jesus, we know, and He is on the throne.

7. Peace, perfect peace, death shad'wing us and ours?
Jesus has vanquished death and all its pow'rs.

8. It is enough: earth's struggles soon shall cease,
And Jesus calls us to Heav'n's perfect peace.

Prayer

"Peace, perfect peace, in this dark world of sin, the blood of Jesus whispers peace within." Heavenly Father, we praise You. We adore Your Holy name for not giving up on us. Praying for peace of mind that passes human understanding as we travel along this "wilderness journey." We pray that You grant us the strength to hold on tight to the end and not give up in any way. May we hear and listen to the blood of Jesus whispering peace within our souls, in the mighty name of Jesus. Amen! Thank You for all Your promises to calm any form of "storm" in our lives. We are casting all our cares upon you, Lord. Please take TOTAL control of ALL that concerns us. May we NEVER feel alone but be reassured that You have promised never to leave or forsake us. Father, You are faithful! Thank You for dying on the cross for our sins. Help us not to nail You on the cross in any way, anymore. Kindly forgive us of ALL our sins and trespasses, in the mighty name of Jesus. Amen!

147

JESUS IS THE ANSWER

You might have been battling with depression for so long and might have tried everything, and nothing seems to be helping. Medications have failed and left you with some form of challenging side effects; you have tried many other things to no avail. You may just be thinking of what to do next or whom to run to. I am recommending **"Dr. Jesus"** to you today. I have tried Him. He is faithful! It is written, *"Oh, taste and see that the LORD is good; Blessed is the man who trusts in Him!"* (Psalm 34:8 NKJV). Come and taste Him today. He is waiting for you with open arms. He knows the details of your life. It is written: *"You know my reproach, my shame, and my dishonor; My adversaries are all before You"* (Psalm 69:19 NKJV). Invite Jesus to walk with you in this wilderness/pilgrim's journey. He knows you very well, and *"He is the way, the truth, and the life"* (John 14:6). He will guide, protect and lead you through, in His holy name. Amen!

Song of Meditation "Jesus is the Answer for The World Today" By Andraé Crouch

Song of Meditation "I Want Jesus To Walk with Me"

African-American Spiritual

1 I want Jesus to walk with me.

I want Jesus to walk with me.

All along my pilgrim journey,

Lord, I want Jesus to walk with me.

2 In my trials, Lord, walk with me.

In my trials, Lord, walk with me.

When my heart is almost breaking,

Lord, I want Jesus to walk with me.

3 When I'm in trouble, Lord, walk with me.

When I'm in trouble, Lord, walk with me.

When my head is bowed in sorrow,

Lord, I want Jesus to walk with me.

OUR BURDEN BEARER

God does not want us to carry the burden/load of sin, guilt, ill health, financial instability, barrenness, marital/family problems or any form of "heavy load" we may be carrying by ourselves. He is our burden bearer. It is written: "*Surely He has borne our griefs and carried our sorrows; Yet we esteemed Him stricken, Smitten by God, and afflicted*" (Isaiah 53:4 NKJV). The Lord has given us the free invitation to call on Him whenever we need Him. He is faithful and ALWAYS available to help and direct us in ALL our ways. It is written: "*Call upon Me in the day of trouble; I will deliver you, and you shall glorify Me*" (Psalm 50:15 NKJV). Every other thing may fail us, but Jesus NEVER fails. It is written: "*For all the promises of God in Him are Yes, and in Him Amen, to the glory of God through us*" (2 Corinthians 1:20 NKJV). "*And being fully convinced that what He had promised He was also able to perform*" (Romans 4:21 NKJV). I am pleading that you try Jesus today. He is able to see you through. Do not be too much in a hurry. Your blessings are on the way. Be patient and DO NOT GIVE UP! "*Wait on the LORD; Be of good courage, and He shall strengthen your heart; Wait, I say, on the LORD*" (Psalm 27:14 NKJV)! You are blessed, in the mighty name of Jesus. Amen!

Song of Meditation "Wait, and Murmur Not" By W. H. Bellamy

1. O troubled heart, there is a home,

Beyond the reach of toil and care;

A home where changes never come;

Who would not fain be resting there?

Chorus

O, wait, meekly wait, and murmur not,

O, wait, meekly wait, and murmur not;

O, wait, O, wait, O wait, and murmur not.

2. Yet when bow'd down beneath the load

By heav'n allow'd, thine earthly lot;

Look up! thoul't reach that blest abode,

Wait, meekly wait, and murmur not.

If in thy path some thorns are found,

O, think who bore them on His brow;

If grief thy sorrowing heart has found,

It reached a holier than thou.

3. Toil on, nor deem, tho' sore it be,

One sigh unheard, one pray'r forgot;

The day of rest will dawn for thee;

Wait, meekly wait, and murmur not.

The challenges of life can make us seek after the worldly "water" like alcohol, promiscuity, drugs, money, fame or any earthly things. I am sorry to say: They will only add to our problems. These forms of "water" will make us "thirst" again. The Lord is willing to give us His divine, holy "water" that will quench our thirst. The Lord will bless us with a fountain of water springing up into everlasting life. He wants us to be honest and approach His throne of grace, just as we are. He is the only one who can quench our "thirst." He will deliver us, in the name of Jesus. Amen! It is written: *"Jesus answered and said to her, "Whoever drinks of this water will thirst again, but whoever drinks of the water that I shall give him will never thirst. But the water that I shall give him will become in him a fountain of water springing up into everlasting life"* (John 4:13-14 NKJV). I pray that we will be honest in our dealings with God and others. May we receive the "living water" and NEVER "thirst" again, in the mighty name of Jesus. Amen!

GOD WILL TURN THINGS AROUND IN YOUR FAVOR

You are a child of God. You mean the whole world to Him. He loves you dearly. He doesn't want you to get discouraged. Be reminded that He died so that you may have life in abundance (John 10:10). He wants you to know that He is turning EVERYTHING around in your favor, in the name of Jesus. Your story will change for the better because God is still on the throne. He loves and cares for you. It is written, *"Behold, I will do a new thing, now it shall spring forth; Shall you not know it? I will even make a road in the wilderness and rivers in the desert"* (Isaiah 43:19 NKJV). May the God of impossibilities visit you today and make ALL your impossible dreams possible, in the name of Jesus. Amen!

REMEMBER! God's plans for you are of good and not evil (Jeremiah 29:11). ALL that God has planned to give you will be delivered, in the mighty name of Jesus. Amen! We just need to be patient. It is written, *"For the LORD God is a sun and shield; The LORD will give grace and glory; No good thing will He withhold from those who walk uprightly"* (Psalm 84:11 NKJV). Darling brother/sister in the Lord, you have read it yourselves that He will Not withhold ANYTHING GOOD from you. Our God is FAITHFUL! It is written, *God is not a man, that He should lie, nor a son of man, that He should repent. Has He said, and will He*

not do? Or has He spoken, and will He not make it good?
(Numbers 23:19 NKJV).

My darling brother/sister in the Lord, there is light at the end of
the tunnel. You are almost there. Labor tends to be very intense
when a woman is about to deliver. You have been so strong, and
you held on till now. The Lord who has kept you this far will
SURELY see you through, in the name of Jesus. Amen! You got
this. You are stronger than you think. Therefore, kindly say NO
to suicide, PLEASE! *"The stone which the builders rejected will
soon become the chief cornerstone"* (Psalm 118:22)! May this be
your experience, in the mighty name of Jesus. Amen!

Song of Meditation "Do Something New in My Life"
Nigerian Praise Song
Do something new in my life
Something new in my life
Something new in my life, I pray
Do something new in my life
Something new in my life
Something new in my life, I pray.

It is written, *"Therefore, if anyone is in Christ, he is a new
creation; old things have passed away; behold, all things have
become new"* (2 Corinthians 5:17 NKJV). May God grant us the
grace to let go of the "old things" and let Him do the COMPLETE

154

"renovation" in our lives, in the name of Jesus. Amen! Dear child of God, I pray that, as from this moment on, God will make EVERYTHING new in your life in the name of Jesus. Everlasting joy will be your portion; the good Lord will take away your sorrow, heal your broken heart and restore your health, finances and fix the void in your life, in the name of Jesus. It is written, *"So, the ransomed of the LORD shall return, and come to Zion with singing, with everlasting joy on their heads. They shall obtain joy and gladness; sorrow and sighing shall flee away"* (Isaiah 51:11 NKJV).

Song of Meditation "I Can See Everything" By Unknown Artiste

I can see everything,

turning around, turning around,

turning around for my favor

May this be your testimony, in the name of Jesus. Amen! As a "born again" child of God, it is time for you to start dressing, walking, talking, dancing and doing EVERYTHING in the perspective of ROYALTY, in the name of Jesus. Your heavenly Father is the King of kings and the Lord of lords. Great change, brother/sister! You have been REDEEMED by the blood of the Lamb; ALL your sins have been washed away, and you are now filled with the Holy Spirit. YOU ARE BORN AGAIN! The ways you once felt (down, anxious, afraid, guilty, low energy, hopeless, lack of interest in things you used to enjoy and other negative feelings) have come to an end. May God grant you the grace to start enjoying meaningful and purposeful life, as from this moment on, in the mighty name of Jesus. Amen!

Song of Meditation "Great Change, Since I was Born" By
Unknown Artiste

1. Great change, since I was born
Great change, since I was born
Great change, since I was born
It is a great change since I been born

2. Things I used to do, I do them no more
Things I used to do, I do them no more
Things I used to do, I do them no more
It is a great change since I was born

3. The way I used to feel, I feel so no more
The way I used to feel, I feel so no more
The way I used to feel, I feel so no more
It is a great change since I was born

GOD IS CALLING YOU OUT OF DARKNESS INTO LIGHT

I t is written: *"But you are a chosen generation, a royal priesthood, a holy nation, His own special people, that you may proclaim the praises of Him who called you out of darkness into His marvelous light"* (1 Peter 2:9 NKJV). Amen! As you are reading this book, I pray that your spirit will be lifted; no depression, no fear or anxiety and NOTHING will "steal" your joy, in the mighty name of Jesus. Amen! The Lord is with you. He will bring you out safely. The enemy might have tried to "dim" your light and put you in "darkness." He has failed, in the name of Jesus because the Lord is calling you out of "darkness" into "light." Just answer the call and follow Him. It is written: *"Then Jesus spoke to them again, saying, "I am the light of the world. He who follows Me shall not walk in darkness, but have the light of life"* (John 8:12 NKJV). It is written: *"For you were once darkness, but now you are light in the Lord. Walk as children of light"* (Ephesians 5:8 NKJV). Therefore, *"Let your light so shine before men, that they may see your good works and glorify your Father in heaven"* (Matthew 5:16 NKJV). I pray that NOTHING will dim the glory of God that is shining in your life as you continue to walk in the light of God, in the mighty name of Jesus. Amen!

The Lord is ready to mend your broken heart. He is ready to trade your sorrow for the joy of the Lord. He is taking away your clothes of shame, pain, ridicule, "barrenness," discouragement, brokenness, hopelessness or whatever "ness" that may be the issue that is weighing you down. He is ready to decorate you with His garment of glory, in the name of Jesus. As of today, ANYTHING causing you sleepless nights is OVER, in the name of Jesus. Allow God to take the sorrow away and trade it with His joy. I pray that, from now on, your sleep will be sweet and peaceful, in the name of Jesus. Amen! It is written: "*When you lie down, you will not be afraid; Yes, you will lie down and your sleep will be sweet*" (Proverbs 3:24 NKJV). No room for depression, in the mighty name of Jesus. Amen! You may be feeling "naked," "cold," and ashamed because of the trauma you have sustained in different forms, from the enemy and his agents.

They might have tried to shatter your dreams. I tell you, they have failed, in the name of Jesus. It is written: "*So, I will restore to you the years that the swarming locust has eaten, the crawling locust, the consuming locust, and the chewing locust, my great army which I sent among you. You shall eat in plenty and be satisfied, and praise the name of the LORD your God, who has dealt wondrously with you; And My people shall never be put to shame. Then you shall know that I am in the midst of Israel: I am the LORD your God and there is no other. My people shall never be put to shame*" (Joel 2:25-32 NKJV). The Lord will replenish ALL that the enemy has stolen in many folds. YOU SHALL NEVER BE PUT TO SHAME, in the mighty name of Jesus. Amen!

Moreover, they might have taken away your beautiful "coat of many colors"; it is just the "coat" that they have taken, not the glory God has given you. They can try, but they will NOT succeed, in the name of Jesus because the glory is in you, not in your "coat." It is secure in the hands of God. NOBODY can take it away. God is the ONLY one in charge of your life, and EVERYTHING about you is safe and secure in His hands. Darling child of God, ALL your disappointments are turning around to be blessings and very important appointments in high places, in the name of Jesus. Amen! Remember that they did this to Joseph: They took off his beautiful coat out of envy, dipped it in the blood and lied that he has been killed (Genesis 37). WHATEVER you are going through will NOT break you but build you. It will NOT kill you, in the name of Jesus. Amen!

It is time to trade your sorrow, your pain, shame, sickness and ALL the challenges for the joy of the Lord. He will help you and see you through. Declare these blessings into your life: *"I shall not die, but live, and declare the works of the Lord"* (Psalm 118:17 NKJV). Maybe it is a new diagnosis that is making you feel so down. It is written: *"When Jesus heard that, He said, 'This sickness is not unto death, but for the glory of God, that the Son of God may be glorified through it'"* (John 11:4 NKJV). I pray that all the challenges surrounding you will not claim your life but the "pain" will turn around to praise, and your sorrow will be traded for the joy of the Lord. Let the enemy know that you have the love of Jesus that has given you the peace that passes human understanding. I tell you; he is in serious trouble! Whether he likes it or not, the joy God has given you has come to stay, in the mighty name of Jesus. Amen!

Song of Meditation "I'm Trading my Sorrow" By Darrell Evans

Song of Meditation "I've Got the Joy, Joy, Joy, Joy" By George W. Cooke

1. I've got the joy, joy, joy, joy,
Down in my heart,
Down in my heart,
Down in my heart;
I've got the joy, joy, joy, joy,
Down in my heart,
Down in my heart to stay.

Chorus
And I'm so happy,
So very happy;
I've got the love of Jesus in my heart.
And I'm so happy,
So very happy,
I've got the love of Jesus in my heart.

2. I've got the peace that passeth understanding,
Down in my heart,
Down in my heart,
Down in my heart;
I've got the peace that passeth understanding,
Down in my heart,
Down in my heart to stay.

3. I've got the love of Jesus, love of Jesus,
   Down in my heart,
   Down in my heart,
   Down in my heart;
I've got the love of Jesus, love of Jesus,
   Down in my heart,
   Down in my heart to stay.

4. There is therefore now no condemnation,
   Down in my heart,
   Down in my heart,
   Down in my heart;
There is therefore now no condemnation,
   Down in my heart,
   Down in my heart to stay.

5. I know that devil doesn't like it, but it's
   Down in my heart,
   Down in my heart,
   Down in my heart
I know that devil doesn't like it, but it's,
   Down in my heart,
   Down in my heart to stay.

GOD IS IN TOTAL CONTROL

When God is the one directing your life, even when things seem to be working against you, have the assurance that God will complete the good work He has started in you, and EVERYTHING WILL BE ALL RIGHT, in the name of Jesus. Joseph's brothers did not know that they were setting him up for greater heights when they sold him as a slave. Fortunately for him and unfortunately for the "enemy of progress," who planned to "abort" his dream, what they meant for evil, God turned it around for good. Hallelujah! So shall your experience be, in the mighty name of Jesus. Amen! God is not done working with you. He is ready to lift you up and make you stand tall, in the name of Jesus. Your enemies will NOT triumph over you. If you are in any form of "pit" right now, DO NOT GIVE UP! It is not the end of your road. The "PALACE" is your "bus stop," and heaven is our final destination (when Jesus comes to take us home).

Brother/sister, EVERLASTING joy will be your portion, in the name of Jesus. Amen! I just want to reinforce God's promises in your life again by repeating this Bible text: *"Behold, I will do a new thing, now it shall spring forth; Shall you not know it? I will even make a road in the wilderness and rivers in the desert"* (Isaiah 43:19 NIV). God is faithful. He has promised to do a new thing in your life and that He will make a way where there seems to be no way. So, darling child of God, help is on the way. DO NOT GIVE UP! Keep pressing on the upward way with the help of God. May your feet be planted on higher ground that God has set for you. The Lord Himself will lift you up and make you stand TALL, in the name of Jesus. You will not fall, and your experience will be from glory to glory, in the name of Jesus. Your head will not hang low except when you are praying to God. By faith, you have been lifted up, and God will not allow ANYONE to pull you down, in the mighty name of Jesus. Amen!

Song of Meditation "Higher Ground" By Johnson Oatman, Jr.

1. I'm pressing on the upward way,
New heights I'm gaining every day;
Still praying as I'm onward bound,
"Lord, plant my feet on higher ground."

Chorus
Lord, lift me up and let me stand,
By faith, on Heaven's tableland,
A higher plane than I have found
Lord, plant my feet on higher ground.

2, My heart has no desire to stay
Where doubts arise and fears dismay;
Though some may dwell where those abound,

My prayer, my aim, is higher ground.

3. I want to live above the world,

Though Satan's darts at me are hurled;

For faith has caught the joyful sound,

The song of saints on higher ground.

4. I want to scale the utmost height

And catch a gleam of glory bright;

But still, I'll pray till heav'n I've found,

"Lord, plant my feet on higher ground."

"If we know how to think, we will know how to thank." No matter what you may be going through, be grateful to God for the gift of life! If we had the opportunity to see the dangers surrounding us, or the grace to see the whole picture of what is happening in our lives, we would appreciate God even more for His protection and for redirecting the arrows of the enemy. The challenges we are facing could be worse. I tell you: It is NOTHING but God's special grace that is keeping us. We say THANK YOU, LORD! Notwithstanding, one can ONLY imagine the pain/heartache you are going through. Let it be known that the Lord who spared your life to see today has not brought you this far to leave you. It is written: *"Being confident of this very thing, that He who has begun a good work in you will complete it until the day of Jesus Christ"* (Philippians 1:6 NKJV).

Apart from COVID-19, "autoimmune disease" (killing ourselves) became a big challenge as well. We know how many lives were lost due to UNNECESSARY discrimination/racism, tribalism, issues with religion and other reasons. Men's hearts were failing them for fear; the lives of animals seemed to be more important than human lives. Racism became "acceptable." It was a BIG mess to the point that it was so difficult to "BREATHE!" We were "choking" ourselves to death for no reason other than prejudice, discrimination and the other aforementioned issues. Unfortunately, there seems to be no sense of remorse. The atmosphere filled with fear, and the whole world was in a great mess. God heard our cries. His mercy kept and protected us. HALLELUJAH! What the Lord has done for you and I, we cannot tell it all. We are not better than the ones who died, but God's grace kept us. He has blessed us to see today. He has taken our fears away. We are "breathing" better now, to His glory, honor and adoration. He is faithful to complete the good work that He has started in all of us. May His grace NEVER depart from us, in the mighty name of Jesus. Amen!

Song of Meditation "He Who Began A Good Work in You"
By Steve Green (1988)

Song of Meditation "What the Lord Has Done for Me" By Unknown Artiste

1. What the Lord has done for me,

I cannot tell it all.

What the Lord has done for me,

I cannot tell it all.

What the Lord has done for me,

I cannot tell it all.

He saved me and washed me, in His blood

Chorus

So, I can shout Hallelujah!

I can shout Hallelujah!

I can shout, praise the Lord.

So, I can shout Hallelujah!

I can shout Hallelujah!

I can shout, praise the Lord.

ALLOW GOD TO BE GOD

The whole world is filled with uncertainties and fear of the unknown. Unfortunately, no one seems to have the solution to the problems yet, except for God. The sad thing is that we are not giving Him the chance to be God in our lives. So, the enemy is attacking us at our "lowest" with anxiety, depression and suicide/homicide. God wants us to surrender EVERYTHING to Him. UNFORTUNATELY, we are distracted, forgetting that the enemy's mission is to kill, steal and destroy, as written in the Bible: *"The thief does not come except to steal, and to kill, and to destroy. I have come that they may have life, and that they may have it more abundantly"* (John 10:10 NKJV). He has stolen our joys in different ways, destroyed relationships by causing division and UNNECESSARY inferiority/superiority complexes that are preventing unity amongst us. It is time to let go and let God be God. It is time to turn everything over to our Savior, so we can smile, and rejoice in the Lord, the rest of our days. May God grant us the grace to let go of EVERYTHING and let Him do the COMPLETE "renovation" in our lives, in the mighty name of Jesus. Amen!

It is written: *"In Him we have redemption through His blood, the forgiveness of sins, according to the riches of His grace"* (Ephesians 1:7 NKJV). Thank God for His love and plan of redemption. The enemy CANNOT triumph over us, in the name

167

of Jesus. Despite our sins and shortcomings, God remains FAITHFUL. He is willing to deliver us from depression, anxiety, any form of plague that may come our way and from all the challenges we may be facing, in the name of Jesus. It is written: *"If My people who are called by My name will humble themselves, and pray and seek My face, and turn from their wicked ways, then I will hear from heaven, and will forgive their sin and heal their land"* (2 Chronicles 7:14 NKJV).

The Bible verse sounds so simple and easy. The truth is, sin can be "sweet," and it is not easy to give up just like that. Moreover, power could be very "intoxicating," and we want to hold on tight to it. So, it is with many other things that may be keeping us from being humble as God wants us to be. I pray that God will deliver us all from WHATEVER may be preventing us from surrendering to Him—things that may be hindering our prayers from being answered and preventing Him from being God in our lives. These may include: "Self." May God heal our lands, souls and body. May He help us to humble ourselves, in the name of Jesus. Amen! It is written: *"He has sent redemption to His people; He has commanded His covenant forever: Holy and awesome is His name"* (Psalm 111:9 NKJV). We are REDEEMED and forgiven, in the mighty name of Jesus. Amen!

Song of Meditation "Redeemed, How I Love to Proclaim It!"
By Fanny Crosby (1882)

1. Redeemed, how I love to proclaim it!

Redeemed by the blood of the Lamb;

Redeemed through His infinite mercy,

His child and forever I am.

Refrain

Redeemed, redeemed,

Redeemed by the blood of the Lamb;

Redeemed, redeemed,

His child and forever I am.

2. Redeemed, and so happy in Jesus,

No language my rapture can tell;

I know that the light of His presence

With me doth continually dwell.

3. I think of my blessed Redeemer,

I think of Him all the day long:

I sing, for I cannot be silent;

His love is the theme of my song.

4. I know I shall see in His beauty

The King in whose law I delight;

Who lovingly guardeth my footsteps,

And giveth me songs in the night.

169

5. I know there's a crown that is waiting

   In yonder bright mansion for me,

And soon, with the spirits made perfect,

   At home with the Lord, I shall be.

I Want God to Use Me

With all that is going on in the world today, I have decided to do something, as little as it may be, in my little corner. I want to be a positive influence on others, by the grace of God, trusting that at least a soul will be blessed/saved through this book, in the name of Jesus. I pray that God will grant me the right attitude toward others and help me in the way I care for my patients. And when I am blessed to open my practice (that I am trusting God for), as a psychiatric mental health nurse practitioner, I will be of service to Him and everyone He will place in my path, in the name of Jesus. Amen! I am pleading to the souls planning to end the journey abruptly: suicide is not the answer to the problems. There is no doubt that the world is full of uncertainties. We hear of wars, rumors of war and many things that may result in anxiety, depression or suicide/homicide if we don't get the necessary help/support on time. Together, we shall walk through the valley in peace if we don't give up. We need each other in this "wilderness journey." It is written: *"For if they fall, one will lift up his companion. But woe to him who is alone when he falls, for he has no one to help him up"* (Ecclesiastes 4:10 NKJV). Once again, I say: Everybody needs someone, and we all need Jesus.

Are you that someone who has no one to lift you up? If it is okay with you, I want to be your friend. I do not have any "magic" to

171

take away your sorrow, pain, discouragement or those things weighing you down, but we both have Jesus, and He is able to see us through, in the name of Jesus. It is written: *"For where two or three are gathered together in My name, I am there in the midst of them"* (Matthew 18:20 NKJV). Feeling of loneliness, rejection, feeling unlovable and being treated differently in a bad way could be very devastating. As children of God, we need to continue to remind ourselves of how much God loves us, how He is coming back to take us home with Him, and we must not forget that we have been instructed to love like He loves.

NO ONE is immune to the challenges of this world. It is written: *"A new commandment I give to you, that you love one another; as I have loved you, that you also love one another. By this all will know that you are My disciples, if you have love for one another"* (John 13:34-35 NKJV). May God help us all! "No one is an island." We need each other. Feel free to reach me via email: peacefulheart.joy@gmail.com. I pray that the peace of God will fill your heart, in the mighty name of Jesus. Amen!

God has given all of us talents, and we can use them to help each other as we travel through this "wilderness journey" I NEED YOU, AS MUCH AS YOU NEED ME. WE NEED EACH OTHER TO SURVIVE. We are all part of God's family. It is written, *"Beloved, let us love one another, for love is of God; and everyone who loves is born of God and knows God"* (1 John 4:7 NKJV). *"Be kindly affectionate to one another with brotherly love, in honor giving preference to one another"* (Romans 12:10

NKJV). REMEMBER: "A tree cannot make a forest." May the good Lord bind us together, with cord that cannot be broken, in the mighty name of Jesus. Amen!

Song of Meditation "I need Thee Every Hour, Most Gracious Lord" By Annie S. Hawks and Robert Lowry (1872).

1. I need Thee ev'ry hour,
Most gracious Lord;
No tender voice like Thine
Can peace afford.

Refrain:
I need Thee, oh, I need Thee;
Ev'ry hour I need Thee;
Oh, bless me now, my Savior,
I come to Thee.

2. I need Thee ev'ry hour,
Stay Thou nearby;
Temptations lose their pow'r
When Thou art nigh.

3. I need Thee ev'ry hour,
In joy or pain;
Come quickly and abide,
Or life is vain.

4. I need Thee ev'ry hour,
Teach me Thy will;
And Thy rich promises
In me fulfill.

CONFUSED ABOUT THE VOICE YOU ARE HEARING?

S ometimes, in this wilderness journey, one may not be able to differentiate the voice of "Eli" from that of God. It is possible to get confused, especially with the "loud noise" around us. May God grant us the clarity and peace of mind needed to hear Him clearly when He speaks to us, in the mighty name of Jesus. Amen! I pray that God will not stop "calling" our names until we answer Him. May we be willing to say, "Speak Lord, for Your servant hears." It is written: *"Now the boy Samuel ministered to the LORD before Eli. And the word of the LORD was rare in those days; there was no widespread revelation. And it came to pass at that time, while Eli was lying down in his place, and when his eyes had begun to grow so dim that he could not see, and before the lamp of God went out in the tabernacle of the LORD where the ark of God was, and while Samuel was lying down, that the LORD called Samuel. And he answered, "Here I am!" So, he ran to Eli and said, "Here I am, for you called me." And he said, "I did not call; lie down again." And he went and lay down. Then the LORD called yet again, "Samuel!" So, Samuel arose and went to Eli, and said, "Here I am, for you called me." He answered, "I did not call, my son; lie down again." (Now Samuel did not yet know the LORD, nor was the word of the LORD yet revealed to him). And the LORD called Samuel again the third time. So, he arose and went to Eli, and said, "Here I am, for you did call me." "Then*

Eli perceived that the LORD had called the boy. Therefore, Eli said to Samuel, 'Go, lie down; and it shall be, if He calls you, that you must say, 'Speak, LORD, for Your servant hears.' So, Samuel went and lay down in his place. Now the LORD came and stood and called as at other times, "Samuel! Samuel!" And Samuel answered, "Speak, for Your servant hears" (1 Samuel 3:1-10 NKJV).

Let me quickly ask you: Are you seeing things that no one else is seeing? Are you hearing voices, and what are they telling you? I want to plead with you: For your safety and that of the people around you, kindly seek professional help if you are experiencing any form of visual or auditory hallucination, please.

Back to the story. Imagine Samuel pretending that he did not hear the call, thinking it was Eli who was calling Him. Samuel was obedient, respectful and he responded throughout the times God was calling him. Moreover, it is a great blessing to have a leader who will direct us to God. Eli, though very tired, did not complain that Samuel was disturbing him. Furthermore, when he finally knew it was God who was calling Samuel, he did not get jealous or wonder why God was calling Samuel, not him. In addition, Eli did not mislead Samuel by advising him to ignore the call and just go back to sleep. Eli took time to study where the voice might be coming from. He knew that Samuel was not familiar with the voice. So, he taught him what to say, "If He calls you, that you must say, 'Speak, LORD, for Your servant hears.'" May your Eli complete and not compete with you, in the mighty name of Jesus. Amen!

I CAN DO ALL THINGS THROUGH CHRIST!

It is written: *"I can do all things through Christ who strengthens me"* (Philippians 4:13 NKJV). We cannot do ANYTHING without Jesus. Before we can effectively be there for one another, we need to pray that God grants us the grace to first love the Lord, then surrender EVERYTHING about us to Him and allow Him to take TOTAL CONTROL of our lives. Then He will help us to love like He loves, see things through His perspective and treat others the way He treats them. Jesus is our best friend and confidant. It is written: *"Greater love has no one than this, than to lay down one's life for his friends"* (John 15:13 NKJV). Jesus died that we may have life (abundant life). He promised to be with us ALWAYS, even to the end of age (Matthew 28:20 NKJV). He is our confidant and our savior.

The enemy loves to torment us with our past mistakes. He loves to lie, make us feel guilty and fearful of approaching God's throne of grace. He is a liar. God has forgiven us our sins and does not remember them anymore. It is written: *"As far as the east is from the west, so far has He removed our transgressions from us"* (Psalm 103:12 NKJV). All we need to do is just invite Him to come into our hearts.

When we have Jesus, we have EVERYTHING. He is FAITHFUL, and He will deliver us in His holy name. Amen! It is written: "*Our soul has escaped as a bird from the snare of the fowlers; The snare is broken, and we have escaped. Our help is in the name of the LORD, who made heaven and earth*" (Psalm 124:7-8 NKJV). Moreover, God says, "*I am the vine; you are the branches. He who abides in Me, and I in him, bears much fruit; for without Me you can do nothing*" (John 15:5 NKJV). With the help of God, depression has to bow, and God will replace it with EVERLASTING joy, and the enemy will not be able to take it away from us. Let us invite Jesus into our hearts/life and give him room to stay FOREVER. With Him on our sides, we are more than conquerors and we are victorious, in the mighty name of Jesus. Amen!

Song of Meditation "Into My Heart" By Unknown Artiste

Into my heart, into my heart

Come into my heart, Lord Jesus

Come in today, come in to stay

Come into my heart, Lord Jesus.

THE LORD WILL FIGHT FOR YOU

Jesus is the solution to our problems. Challenges of today may make one feel so stressed and think the whole world is collapsing all around. Looking in front, the Red Sea is in sight; looking at the back, the "Egyptian army"; and one feels surrounded with dangers, left, right and center. It could feel like one is growing amongst the thorns, and one may feel choked up if something is not done fast. Hold on tight, dear brother/sister in the Lord. It is written: *"And Moses said to the people, "Do not be afraid. Stand still, and see the salvation of the LORD, which He will accomplish for you today. For the Egyptians whom you see today, you shall see again no more forever"* (Exodus 14:13 NKJV). The good Lord who delivered the Israelites from the hand of their enemies is still alive. He is more than able to see you through, in the name of Jesus. He will part your "red sea"; you will walk on "dry land" and the "waters" will not close up on you, in the name of Jesus. Amen! The "pit" you are in is not going to turn to your "grave." You are going to come out alive and well, in the mighty name of Jesus. Amen!

Our miracle-working God will perform His miracles in your life. Let us agree with the host of heaven that your mountains are leveled today. The Lord will make a way out of no way, and your testimonies will be full, in the name of Jesus. Amen! Let us keep admonishing ourselves and be reminded that Jesus is coming,

VERY SOON. In addition, we are to continue to encourage one another because all of us are on different kinds of battlefields. Everyone has his or her own challenges, and we all have our stories to tell. It is written: *"The LORD will fight for you, and you shall hold your peace"* (Exodus 14:14 NKJV). God will continue to fight our battles for us, in the name of Jesus. Amen! He has never lost ANY, and yours will not be an exception, in the name of Jesus. He fought for Jehoshaphat (2 Chronicles 20:1-30). The God of Jehoshaphat is still alive and His message for you today is: *"Be not afraid* (PUT YOUR NAME HERE) *nor dismayed by reason of this great multitude; for **THE BATTLE IS NOT YOURS, BUT GOD'S"*** (2 Chronicles 20:15; emphasis added). We are on the battlefield, but God is the one fighting the battles. WE are winners, in the mighty name of Jesus. Amen!

Song of Meditation "I am On the Battlefield for My Lord"
By E. V. Banks, Sylvanna Bell

I am on the battlefield for my Lord,
I'm on the battlefield for my Lord;
And I promised Him that I would serve Him till I die.
I am on the battlefield for my Lord.

1. I was alone and idle,
I was a sinner too,
I heard a voice from heaven
Say there is work to do,
I took the Master's hand,
And I joined the Christian band,
I'm on the battlefield for my Lord.

2. I left my friends and kindred
Bound for the Promised Land,
The grace of God upon me,
The Bible in my hand,
In distant lands I trod,
Crying, sinner, come to God,
I'm on the battlefield for my Lord.

3. Now when I met my Savior,
I met Him with a smile,
He healed my wounded spirit,
And owned me as His child,
Around the throne of grace,
He appoints my soul a place,
I'm on the battlefield for my Lord.

TURN IT OVER TO JESUS

We cannot do anything on our own without the help of God. Disappointments may come from every angle of life—turning to the right, left and center. To family members or friends, this may sometimes add to the pain and the burdens we bear. But when we look up to the Author and Finisher of our faith, we receive comfort, peace, love and all that our hearts long for. Our help comes from the Lord. It is written: *"I will lift up my eyes to the hills. From whence comes my help? My help comes from the LORD, who made heaven and earth. He will not allow your foot to be moved; He who keeps you will not slumber. Behold, He who keeps Israel shall neither slumber nor sleep. The LORD is your keeper; The LORD is your shade at your right hand. The sun shall not strike you by day, nor the moon by night. The LORD shall preserve you from all evil;*

He shall preserve your soul. The LORD shall preserve your going out and your coming in

From this time forth, and even forevermore" (Psalm 121:1-8 NKJV). So, shall it be, in the name of Jesus. Amen!

What a MIGHTY God we serve! May He grant us the grace to be able to COMPLETELY surrender EVERYTHING to Him. He is more than able to see us through, in the name of Jesus. Amen! He is the King of kings and the Lord of lords! It is written: *"Who is this King of glory? The LORD strong and mighty, the LORD mighty in battle. Lift up your heads, O ye gates; even lift them up, ye everlasting doors; and the King of glory shall come in. Who is this King of glory? The* LORD *of hosts, He is the King of glory. Selah"* (Psalm 24:8-10 KJV). Let us continue to fight the battle of faith. With God on our sides, we are more than conquerors. I pray that the good Lord will continue to guide and protect all of us unto the end. May we be counted worthy to reign eternally with Him, in the mighty name of Jesus. Amen!

Song of Meditation "Turn It Over to Jesus" By Unknown Artiste

Turn It Over to Jesus

Turn It Over to Jesus

Turn It Over to Jesus

So, you can smile the rest of your days.

I AM NOT FORGOTTEN!

N o matter the challenges of life, we serve a faithful God who loves and cares for us. He will make our "righteousness" go forth as brightness and our salvation as a "lamp" that burns. The Lord will change our names for good, and victory is ours, in the mighty name of Jesus. Amen! It is written: *"For Zion's sake I will not hold My peace, and for Jerusalem's sake I will not rest, until her righteousness goes forth as brightness, and her salvation as a lamp that burns. The Gentiles shall see your righteousness, and all kings your glory. You shall be called by a new name, which the mouth of the LORD will name"* (Isaiah 62:1-2 NKJV). Claim the promises and put your name where you have Zion and Jerusalem. Moreover, *"You shall also be a crown of glory in the hand of the LORD, and a royal diadem in the hand of your God. You shall no longer be termed Forsaken, nor shall your land anymore be termed Desolate; But you shall be called Hephzibah, and your land Beulah; For the LORD delights in you, and your land shall be married"* (Isaiah 62:3-4 NKJV). I pray that all of these blessings will be ours forever, in the mighty name of Jesus. Amen!

Mary Ann Baker wrote a song in 1874. It seems she had seen the vision of everything happening in the world today: "Master, the tempest is raging! The billows are tossing high! The sky is o'er shadowed with blackness. No shelter or help is nigh." I don't know about you, but I have asked the "forbidden" question,

"WHY, GOD?" Several times due to fear, failures, heartache, rejection, concerns and many other reasons, you may be asking the same or similar questions today. Some of us are very weary, worn out and tired of moving on. I pray that the giver of peace will continue to grant us the peace that passes human understanding, may He continue to remind us of how much he cares and help us NEVER to give up, in the mighty name of Jesus. Amen!

Song of Meditation "Does Jesus Care?" By Frank E. Graeff (1901)

1. Does Jesus care when my heart is pained
Too deeply for mirth or song;
As the burdens press, and the cares distress,
And the way grows weary and long?

Refrain:
O, yes, He cares- I know He cares!
His heart is touched with my grief;
When the days are weary, the long nights dreary,
I know my Savior cares.

2. Does Jesus care when my way is dark
With a nameless dread and fear?
As the daylight fades into deep night shades,
Does He care enough to be near?

3. Does Jesus care when I've tried and failed
To resist some temptation strong;
When for my deep grief there is no relief,
Though my tears flow all the night long?

4. Does Jesus care when I've said goodbye
To the dearest on earth to me,
And my sad heart aches till it nearly breaks—
Is it aught to Him? does He see?

We sometimes wonder if God has forgotten or forsaken us. We question if He really cares. We are so confused, and we imagine how Jesus can really be "sleeping" when "each moment is so madly threatening, 'a grave in the angry deep.'" Loved ones dying, job instabilities, bills piling up with no hope of how to pay them, plagues of all kinds, medical reports, not to mention the divorce rate and challenging children or parents. The truth is: God cares, and He is more than able to see us through, in the name of Jesus. It is written: *"Behold, He who keeps Israel shall neither slumber nor sleep"* (Psalm 121:4 NKJV). He is not sleeping. He is in TOTAL CONTROL! Meditate on the words/lyrics of the song below or sing it if you know it. May your soul be refreshed, nourished, lifted, renewed and blessed, as you sing/meditate, in the name of Jesus. Be assured that Jesus cares despite the burdens, distress, pain or grief. Let it be known to you today, "His heart is touched with your grief" and you are not forsaken. I pray that God will calm the storm and "command" that peace be still, in the mighty name of Jesus. Amen!

Song of Meditation "Master, The Tempest Is Raging" By Mary Ann Baker (1874)

1. Master, the tempest is raging!

The billows are tossing high!

The sky is o'er shadowed with blackness.

No shelter or help is nigh.

Carest thou not that we perish?

How canst thou lie asleep

When each moment so madly is threat'ning

A grave in the angry deep

Chorus:

The winds and the waves shall obey thy will:

Peace, be still, peace be still.

Whether the wrath of the storm-tossed sea

Or demons or men or whatever it be,

No waters can swallow the ship where lies

The Master of ocean and earth and skies.

They all shall sweetly obey thy will:

Peace, be still; peace, be still.

They all shall sweetly obey thy will:

Peace, peace, be still.

2. Master, with anguish of spirit

I bow in my grief today.

The depths of my sad heart are troubled.

Oh, waken and save, I pray!

Torrents of sin and of anguish

Sweep o'er my sinking soul,

And I perish! I perish! Dear Master.

Oh, hasten and take control!

3. Master, the terror is over.

The elements sweetly rest.

Earth's sun in the calm lake is mirrored,

And heaven's within my breast.

Linger, O blessed Redeemer!

Leave me alone no more,

And with joy, I shall make the blest harbor

And rest on the blissful shore.

ABOUT TO BE BLESSED

We may be feeling "crippled," forgotten, and we may be thinking that all hope is lost. This is when Jesus shows up in a miraculous way to rescue us. He has special and divine ways of showing us His love, mercy/grace and faithfulness. Remember the story of Mephibosheth, the son of Jonathan. He was crippled because he was MISTAKENLY dropped. It is written: *"Jonathan, Saul's son, had a son who was lame in his feet. He was five years old when the news about Saul and Jonathan came from Jezreel; and his nurse took him up and fled. And it happened, as she made haste to flee, that he fell and became lame. His name was Mephibosheth"* (2 Samuel 4:4 NKJV). Darling brother/sister, I don't know who "dropped" you. I have no idea if the "drop" was a mistake or intentional. Whatever the case, just know that the Lord has not forgotten you. He cares, and He is NEVER late. He is ALWAYS on time. Your helper is already searching for you. Be patient and DO NOT GIVE UP! Help is on the way.

It is written: *"Now David said, "Is there still anyone who is left of the house of Saul, that I may show him kindness for Jonathan's sake?" And there was a servant of the house of Saul whose name was Ziba. So, when they had called him to David, the king said to him, "Are you Ziba?" He said, "At your service!" Then the king said, "Is there not still someone of the house of Saul, to whom I may show the kindness of God?" And Ziba said to the king,*

189

"There is still a son of Jonathan who is lame in his feet." So, the king said to him, "Where is he?" And Ziba said to the king, "Indeed he is in the house of Machir the son of Ammiel, in Lo Debar." Then King David sent and brought him out of the house of Machir, the son of Ammiel, from Lo Debar (2 Samuel 9:1-5 NKJV).

God will surprise you beyond your imagination. Your helper will soon find you and "shower" you with an abundance of blessings, in the mighty name of Jesus. Amen! It is written: *"Now when Mephibosheth the son of Jonathan, the son of Saul, had come to David, he fell on his face and prostrated himself. Then David said, 'Mephibosheth?' And he answered, 'Here is your servant!' So, David said to him, 'Do not fear, for I will surely show you kindness for Jonathan your father's sake, and will restore to you all the land of Saul your grandfather; and you shall eat bread at my table continually.' Then he bowed himself, and said, 'What is your servant, that you should look upon such a dead dog as I"* (2 Samuel 9:6-8 NKJV)? I don't know the names you have been calling yourself. Mephibosheth called himself "a dead dog" but God called him a very important person—one who eats at the same table with the king.

Our God is awesome! It is written: *"He raises the poor from the dust and lifts the beggar from the ash heap, to set them among princes and make them inherit the throne of glory. For the pillars of the earth are the LORD's, and He has set the world upon them"* (1 Samuel 2:8 NKJV). God will raise you up too, in the name of

Jesus. I pray the divine turn around God is about to do in your life will make you dance like David danced. Any form of "deformity" in your life has ended, in the name of Jesus. No more stagnation, setback, poverty or any form of suffering, in the mighty name of Jesus. The Lord has given us the invitation to come just as we are, to eat "bread" at his table for the rest of our lives. Our condition has changed for good; we are victorious, in the mighty name of Jesus. Amen!

Song of Meditation "He Brought Me to His Banqueting Table" By Unknown Artiste

1. He brought me to, His banqueting table,

His banner over me is love.

He brought me to, His banqueting table,

His banner over me is love.

He brought me to, His banqueting table,

His banner over me is love.

His banner, over me, is love.

2. I am my beloved's, and He is mine

His banner over me is love,

I am my beloved's, and He is mine

His banner over me is love,

I am my beloved's, and He is mine

His banner over me is love,

His banner, over me, is love.

3. Jesus is the Rock of my salvation,

His banner over me is love.

Jesus is the Rock of my salvation,

His banner over me is love.

Jesus is the Rock of my salvation,

His banner over me is love.

His banner, over me, is love.

4. God is my Father and I'm His child,

His banner over me is love.

God is my Father and I'm His child,

His banner over me is love.

God is my Father and I'm His child,

His banner over me is love.

His banner, over me, is love.

Prayer

Heavenly Father, thank You for Your love, protection, provision and the promise that You will come back and take us home with You, where there will be no more fear, sorrow, heartache, sickness, death, crying, famine, weather disasters, COVID-19 or any form of plaque. I am humbly knocking on your door of mercy, Father; kindly calm the storms in our lives. I pray that the "winds" and the "waves" will obey Your will, loving Lord. I say, "Peace, be still," in the mighty name of Jesus! Help us to cast our cares upon You. Give us the grace to know and accept that You are in TOTAL control of our lives, knowing You care. May we learn to cast our cares upon You, most especially when we don't know what to do. Grant us Your divine grace to be able to let go and let You take TOTAL control of our lives, in the mighty name of Jesus. Amen!

Song of Meditation "I'll Cast All My Cares Upon You" By Kelly Willard

GOD IS AWARE OF YOUR TRIALS

As I travel through the "wilderness journey," I realize that our trials are not strange to God. He is aware, and He has "ordained" everything we must experience in life to be able to get us to where He wants us to be. I don't know your story, but the fact that you have been through or just passing through your own form of "wilderness journey" and you are still alive, I want to congratulate you because, "as long as there is life, there is hope." You are NEVER alone. The good Lord who has brought you this far will not leave you. I pray that your story will end well and that ALL that the enemy has stolen from you will be replenished in many folds, in the mighty name of Jesus. Amen! You will not die in the "wilderness." You will make it to the Glory Land and testify of the goodness of God, in the mighty name of Jesus. Amen!

The "load" we carry during our trials may be very heavy, especially when God has decided He will NOT share His Glory with ANYONE! He might make EVERYONE turn their back on you. The long and lonely road could be very depressing. At your lowest, when the "rain" is pouring down so hard on you, God may make the ones who are supposed to give you an "umbrella" very far from you or unavailable. You may feel all alone, rejected, frustrated, "naked," very cold and confused. Thank God for Jesus;

Our shepherd, Rock of Ages and our shelter in the time of storm. He will shield and protect us. We are secure in Him. I will tell you that if your security is in your parents, siblings, spouse, children, friends, career, level of education, money, possessions, the so-called prayer partners who may be "wolves in sheep clothing" or ANYTHING other than JESUS, we may be setting ourselves up for trouble, failure and big disappointments. Let your security be in God; He is faithful!

It is written: *"My soul, wait silently for God **ALONE**, for my expectation is from Him. He only is my rock and my salvation; He is my defense; I shall not be moved. In God is my salvation and my glory; The rock of my strength, and my refuge, is in God. Trust in Him at all times, you people; Pour out your heart before Him; God is a refuge for us. Selah. Surely men of low degree are a vapor, Men of high degree are a lie; If they are weighed on the scales, they are altogether lighter than vapor. Do not trust in oppression, nor vainly hope in robbery; if riches increase, do not set your heart on them. God has spoken once, twice I have heard this: That power belongs to God. Also, to You, O Lord, belongs mercy; For You render to each one according to his work"* (Psalm 62:5-12 NKJV; emphasis added). I have had enough disappointments in life to know that *"Jesus is the way, the truth and life"* (John 14:6). He will never fail. All other ground, brother/sister, is sinking sand! Don't waste your time and energy on building your hope on ANYTHING/ANYONE, but JESUS, HIS BLOOD AND RIGHTEOUSNESS! He is faithful, He will

NEVER fail, and He is able to carry you through. You are victorious, in the mighty name of Jesus. Amen!

Song of Meditation "My Hope Is Built on Nothing Less" By Edward Mote (1834)

1. My hope is built on nothing less
Than Jesus' blood and righteousness;
I dare not trust the sweetest frame,
But wholly lean on Jesus' name.

Chorus:
On Christ the solid rock I stand;
All other ground is sinking sand.
On Christ the solid rock I stand,
All other ground is sinking sand.

2. When darkness seems to veil His face,
I rest on His unchanging grace;
In every high and stormy gale
My anchor holds within the veil.

3. His oath His covenant and blood
Support me in the 'whelming flood:
When all around my soul gives way,
He then is all my hope and stay.

4. When the last trumpet's voice shall sound,
O may I then in Him be found.
Clothed in his righteousness alone,
Faultless to stand before his throne.

196

GOD IS A JEALOUS GOD

God is a jealous God (Exodus 34:14), and He will **NOT** share His glory with ANYONE, "*I am the LORD, that is My name; and My glory I will not give to another, nor My praise to carved images*" (Isaiah 42:8 NKJV). Notwithstanding, He has His children/representatives here on earth. We are His ears, hands, legs and everything. At His own time, He will bring His "representatives" into your life, and it will be very apparent that they are Godsent—very AMAZING people, you can call at any time of the day, and they will motivate, speak words of comfort, assure you, pray with you and help put a smile back on your face, through the help of God. These types of people are not easy to come by.

The ones who will judge, mock and ridicule you are not too far away. After making the mistake of talking to them, you might wonder whether they had been waiting for the opportunity to be very mean to you. It could have been that these people are the types that love to claim glories that are not theirs. So, God will allow them to disappoint you. Life experiences may teach us how to cultivate Jehoshaphat's principle of "running to the throne of God and not to earthly men, who may not be reliable." Life disappointments may result in fear, distrust, shame and hopelessness. We may become hesitant to share our concerns with people. So, we may decide to obtain a very good "veil/makeup," the "right size" for our faces that would blend PERFECTLY. Jesus is all we need. He is our source of joy, our lives and our all in all.

Let us use the analogy of how we care for our clothes. Some we can wash in the machine with the right settings, while some are dry clean only. If we make the mistake of washing what is "dry clean only" in the washing machine, we know it is a great risk we are taking. The cloth may be damaged. So, it is with talking with people. May God grant us the grace to be able to know which of our issues are "dry clean only" and the ones to "wash in the machine," in the mighty name of Jesus. Amen!

Song of Meditation "Jesus is All the World to Me" By Dino Kartsonakis (1904)

1. Jesus is all the world to me,
My life, my joy, my all;
He is my strength from day to day,
Without Him I would fall.
When I am sad to Him I go,
No other one can cheer me so;
When I am sad He makes me glad,
He's my Friend.

2. Jesus is all the world to me,
And true to Him I'll be;
O how could I this Friend deny,
When He's so true me?
Following Him I know I'm right,
He watches o'er me Day and night;
Following Him by day and night,
He's my Friend.

3. Jesus is all the world to me,
I want no better friend;
I trust Him now, I'll trust when
Life's fleeting days shall end.
Beautiful life with such a Friend;
Beautiful life that has no end;
Eternal life, eternal joy,
He's my Friend.

OUR LIVES BELONG TO GOD

No matter the challenges, we must not forget that we are not the owner of our lives. So, we cannot take it anyhow. They belong to God. It is written: *"For if we live, we live to the Lord; and if we die, we die to the Lord. Therefore, whether we live or die, we are the Lord's"* (Romans 14:8 NKJV). In addition, we are to *"Know that the LORD, He is God; It is He who has made us, and not we ourselves; We are His people and the sheep of His pasture"* (Psalm 100:3 NKJV). *"Or do you not know that your body is the temple of the Holy Spirit who is in you, whom you have from God, and you are not your own"* (1 Corinthians 6:19 NKJV)? I am happy to inform you that the Lord protected me from dying in the "wilderness." He found me, gave me His "divine GPS" and He helped me find my way. I say glory to the Father, the Son and the Holy Spirit. Be patient. He will find you too and set your feet on the right part, in the mighty name of Jesus. Amen!

Song of Meditation "Take my Life and Let It Be" By Frances Ridley Havergal (1874)

1. Take my life and let it be
consecrated, Lord, to thee.
Take my moments and my days;
let them flow in endless praise,
let them flow in endless praise.

2. Take my hands and let them move
at the impulse of thy love.
Take my feet and let them be
swift and beautiful for thee,
swift and beautiful for thee.

3. Take my voice and let me sing
always, only, for my King.
Take my lips and let them be
filled with messages from thee,
filled with messages from thee.

4. Take my silver and my gold;
not a mite would I withhold.
Take my intellect and use
every power as thou shalt choose,
every power as thou shalt choose.

5. Take my will and make it thine;
it shall be no longer mine.
Take my heart it is thine own;
it shall be thy royal throne,
it shall be thy royal throne.

6. Take my love; my Lord, I pour
at thy feet its treasure store.
Take myself, and I will be
ever, only, all for thee,
ever, only, all for thee.

Bring your burdens to Calvary and be reminded that Jesus is ready to help take the weight off. He is the one in charge of our tomorrow. It is written, *"Come to Me, all you who labor and are heavy laden, and I will give you rest. Take My yoke upon you and learn from Me, for I am gentle and lowly in heart, and you will find rest for your souls. For My yoke is easy and My burden is light"* (Matthew 11:28-30 NKJV). It is time for all of us to let go and let God take TOTAL control of ALL that concerns us. Come just as you are to Jesus. The way we handle our issues determines the outcome. Anxiety is a big thing in the world today. No one knows what the next minute holds. The good news is that we know who is in TOTAL control of our lives and our tomorrow. Therefore, we can remind ourselves that because He lives, we can face tomorrow. He loves us so much as filthy and unworthy as we may be, His wonderous love/grace abounds. May He help take all our fears away, in the name of Jesus. Amen!

Song of Meditation "I Know Not Why God's Wondrous Grace" By Daniel Webster Whittle (1883)

1. I know not why God's wondrous grace,
   To me he hath made known,
   Nor why unworthy Christ in love
   Redeemed me for his own.

REFRAIN

But 'I know whom I have believed,
And am persuaded that he is able.
To keep that which I've committed,
Unto him against that day.

2. I know not how this saving faith,
To me he did impart,
Nor how believing in his word,
Wrought peace within my heart.

3. I know not how the Spirit moves,
Convincing men of sin,
Revealing Jesus through the Word,
Creating faith in him.

4. I know not what of good or ill
May be reserved for me,
Of weary ways or golden days,
Before his face I see.

5. I know not when my Lord may come,
At night or noonday fair,
Nor if I'll walk the vale with him,
Or meet him in the air.

ENCOURAGING BIBLE VERSES (ANTI-DEPRESSANTS)

Treatment of depression is not a one-size-fits-all. What works for "A" may not work for "B." That is why we keep trying until goals are met, and the patient can verbalize that they are feeling better and that the plan of care is working for them. Some patients prefer medications, while some do not. Everyone has his or her ways of coping with stress. If what works for you is not going to cause you or people around you any harm, we try to work with you, acknowledging that we have patients from different cultures, races, nationalities, religions and beliefs, just to mention a few. If you are the type who believes in the Bible blessings, or you want to combine the scriptures with your other plans of care (medication/counseling therapy), you can do so. The scriptures have no adverse effects and no negative interactions with other plans of care. It is not contraindicated. In addition, if you have tried every other thing and they have failed, try Jesus and His words through the scriptures. These are AMAZING anti-depressants that we are yet to utilize well. It is free and easily accessible. No prescription is needed. All you need is little faith like that of a mustard seed. It is written: *"So Jesus said to them, 'Because of your unbelief; for assuredly, I say to you, if you have faith as a mustard seed, you will say to this mountain, Move from here to there,' and it will move; and nothing will be impossible for you'"* (Matthew 17:20 NKJV).

204

Some of the scriptures are listed below. You can take as many as you want in a day. They are available in audio and hard copy. It is better to take for life. WARNING! Excessive use of the scriptures may result in: overflowing blessings, joy, peace of mind and many miracles. It is written: *"Your word is a lamp to my feet and a light to my path. I am afflicted very much; Revive me, O LORD, according to Your word"* (Psalm 119:105 &107 NKJV). So, brother/sister in the Lord, enjoy getting "lifted" with the word of God. May it bring healing to your soul, in the name of Jesus. Amen!

"Fear not, for I am with you; Be not dismayed, for I am your God. I will strengthen you,
Yes, I will help you, I will uphold you with My righteous right hand" (Isaiah 41:10 NKJV).

"Is this not the fast that I have chosen: To loose the bonds of wickedness, to undo the heavy burdens, to let the oppressed go free, and that you break every yoke?" (Isaiah 58:6 NKJV)

"Do not fear, for you will not be ashamed; Neither be disgraced, for you will not be put to shame; For you will forget the shame of your youth, and will not remember the reproach of your widowhood anymore. For your Maker is your husband, the LORD of hosts is His name; and your Redeemer is the Holy One of Israel; He is called the God of the whole earth. For the LORD has called you like a woman forsaken and grieved in spirit, like a youthful wife when you were refused," Says your God. *"For a mere*

205

moment I have forsaken you, but with great mercies I will gather you. With a little wrath I hid My face from you for a moment; But with everlasting kindness I will have mercy on you," Says the LORD, your Redeemer" (Isaiah 54:4-8 NKJV).

"For the mountains shall depart and the hills be removed, but my kindness shall not depart from you, nor shall my covenant of peace be removed, says the LORD, who has mercy on you. O, you afflicted one, tossed with tempest, and not comforted, behold, I will lay your stones with colorful gems, and lay your foundations with sapphires. I will make your pinnacles of rubies, your gates of crystal, and all your walls of precious stones. All your children shall be taught by the LORD, and great shall be the peace of your children. In righteousness you shall be established; you shall be far from oppression, for you shall not fear; and from terror, for it shall not come near you. Indeed, they shall surely assemble, but not because of Me. Whoever assembles against you shall fall for your sake. "Behold, I have created the blacksmith who blows the coals in the fire,

Who brings forth an instrument for his work; And I have created the spoiler to destroy. No weapon formed against you shall prosper, and every tongue which rises against you in judgment

You shall condemn. This is the heritage of the servants of the LORD, and their righteousness is from Me," Says the LORD" (Isaiah 54:10-17 NKJV).

"But now, thus says the LORD, who created you, O Jacob, and He who formed you, O Israel:

"Fear not, for I have redeemed you; I have called you by your name; You are Mine. When you pass through the waters, I will be with you; And through the rivers, they shall not overflow you.

When you walk through the fire, you shall not be burned, nor shall the flame scorch you.

For I am the LORD your God, The Holy One of Israel, your Savior; I gave Egypt for your ransom, Ethiopia and Seba in your place. Since you were precious in My sight, you have been honored, and I have loved you; Therefore, I will give men for you and people for your life. Fear not, for I am with you; I will bring your descendants from the east and gather you from the west" (Isaiah 43:1-5 NKJV). May you be encouraged today and always, in the name of Jesus. Amen!

NOTHING CAN SEPARATE US FROM GOD'S LOVE

The Lord wants you to come to Him just as you are. He does not require that you put up your "best" before coming to His special throne of grace, where His heavenly blessings abound. Hallelujah! Our sins/blemishes cannot separate us from His love. It is written: *"For I am persuaded that neither death nor life, nor angels nor principalities nor powers, nor things present nor things to come, nor height nor depth, nor any other created thing, shall be able to separate us from the love of God which is in Christ Jesus our Lord"* (Romans 8:38-39 NKJV). Jesus is saying to you today: *"Come now, and let us reason together," Says the LORD "though your sins are like scarlet, they shall be as white as snow; Though they are red like crimson, they shall be as wool"* (Isaiah 1:18 NKJV). It is written: *"All that the Father gives Me will come to me, and the one who comes to me I will by no means cast out"* (John 6:37 NKJV). God is inviting us to come, as wretched, lost and fearful as we may be. He is our shield and protector. May we continue to enjoy this AMAZING grace and UNCONDITIONAL love of God, in the mighty name of Jesus. Amen!

Song of Meditation "Amazing Grace" By John Newton (1779)

1. Amazing grace! How sweet the sound
   That saved a wretch like me!
   I once was lost, but now am found;
   Was blind, but now I see.

2. 'Twas grace that taught my heart to fear,
   And grace my fears relieved;
   How precious did that grace appear
   The hour I first believed.

3. Through many dangers, toils, and snares,
   I have already come;
   'Tis grace hath brought me safe thus far,
   And grace will lead me home.

4. The Lord has promised good to me,
   His Word my hope secures;
   He will my Shield and Portion be,
   As long as life endures.

5. Yea, when this flesh and heart shall fail,
   And mortal life shall cease,
   I shall possess, within the veil,
   A life of joy and peace.

6. The earth shall soon dissolve like snow,
   The sun forbear to shine;
   But God, who called me here below,
   Will be forever mine.

7. When we've been there ten thousand years,
   Bright shining as the sun,
   We've no less days to sing God's praise
   Than when we'd first begun.

EVERYONE HAS HIS OR HER DOWN MOMENTS

Darling brother/sister in the Lord, you are not alone in this "wilderness journey." Like I have said before, we all have "issues." There is a Yoruba adage that says, "Tí a bá pé mítìnì (meeting) ìyà, a má a mo, alága ìsé." Meaning: If we are to have a round table talk and share our stories, you and I will appreciate whatever load we are carrying because we may realize that one load is heavier than the other. What we are calling a "heavy load" may not be as heavy compared to what others are caring about. Many are in pain, but just like you and I, they have their fitted "veils/makeup," which is making it very difficult for anyone to know. I am not underestimating your pain or comparing it with others, please. Your pain is WHATEVER you call it. I am just trying to encourage you not to feel that you are alone in this. The challenges will not break you, but they will build you by the grace of God. The Lord is with you. He will make a way of escape, in the name of Jesus (1 Corinthians 10:13). Amen! Another Yoruba adage says: "Birds do sweat too, but their feathers are what is preventing us from seeing the sweat. May we be covered under the wings of God, in the name of Jesus. Amen!

What is the level of your pain? Your threshold for pain is different from others. It's only you and God who have the idea of how much you can bear and the weight of pain you are carrying. He is right there with you, upholding you with His right hand of

211

righteousness, in the name of Jesus. Amen! In the medical "world," a patient's pain is whatever he/she calls it. The providers have to respect that and develop a patient-centered management plan, not a "one-size-fits-all" plan. It will be very nice to have this type of respect and "plan of care" in God's "emergency room" (the church) as well. Notwithstanding, fellow brother/sister in the Lord, if no one understands your pain, Jesus does, and He will take very good care of you. No matter the level of your pain, I want you to know that God can and will see you through, in the name of Jesus. Amen! The truth is that the situation could be worse. The goal of the enemy is to destroy God's children. You are alive today, blessed be the name of the Lord. The Yoruba people say: "Dupe ti e." meaning, "Be thankful in whatever situation you find yourself." **May the good Lord soothe your pain. May His blood, on the cross of Calvary, be the "balm of Gilead/analgesia" and take your pain away, in the mighty name of Jesus. Amen!**

You will be surprised that some doctors, other healthcare providers, including mental health care providers and spiritual leaders, also have their challenging moments. Some psychiatrists may be taking one form of antianxiety/antidepressant medication/s because they are human too. No one is immune to the challenges of this world. Many doctors have committed suicide when they couldn't take it anymore. I have heard of pastors who committed suicide as well. So, ANYONE can trip at any time. It's only God who can help/save us all. Moreover, the presidents, kings, chiefs and the "rich" people have their own "makeups" of "it is well" also. Our leaders need our prayers and support as much as we need theirs. Just bear it in mind that EVERYONE has his/her challenges. Be nice to everyone you meet and try to be a blessing, not a problem/pain, please. I pray that God will teach us how to be there for one another. May our living never be in vain, but may our lives touch at least a soul for the Lord as we travel along this "wilderness journey" in a positive and meaningful way. May we still have the "sweet-smelling aroma," even under pressure, in the name of Jesus. Amen!

Song of Meditation "If I Can Help Somebody" By Mahalia Jackson (1996)

THERE ARE NO HOOPS WITH GOD

God knows that you are the right candidate to be married to that "difficult" spouse. He knows that no one else can handle that disobedient and wayward child and bring him/her back to God. God knows you are the one with the level of patience, who can deal with that very difficult boss or that co-worker, who is ready to step on your nerves, putting you on guard, through the help of God, so that he/she will not have easy access to step on those precious nerves. God knows that He can use you to touch the life of that professor at school, whose goal is to keep failing students. He is counting on you for that patient who is so frustrated and overwhelmed with his or her health condition and angry, not necessarily at you but at the situation, crying out for help and compassion. This patient needs a provider like you who will be sympathetic/empathetic enough to understand the reason/s behind the negative behavior. The patient needs that sweet, loving and caring provider who has a BIG HEART. One who will not judge but try to help him/her smile again, even if the condition is terminal; the caring provider who will help the patient die a peaceful death; that care provider who will hold the hand of a dying patient, sing and speak words of comfort that are in line with the patient's faith and beliefs. Yes, you! You may be the last person God is relying on to make a positive influence in the life of His precious child. You may be the last "bus stop" before the patient breaths his/her last breath. Can God depend on you?

Song of Meditation "You Can Depend on Me, Jesus" By Andréa Crouch

I had the opportunity of working with a dying patient as a hospice nurse. This patient had no family to depend on for support. The "patient load" then, was one patient per nurse, and the patients could receive care in the comfort of their homes, assisted living, nursing home or anywhere the patient felt comfortable. This patient was singing with a weak voice so, I joined, holding the patient's hand as tolerated and permitted. It was an amazing experience to see the smooth, happy and struggle-free transition into glory. It was like singing a lullaby to a child who is about to sleep. I thank God for the opportunity given me to be there for the patients He sent my way. May the Lord depend on us, may we be His good ambassadors, in the name of Jesus. Amen!

In the medical world today, it could be very challenging to do all we want to do for our patients due to time constraints, as evidenced by the "patient load." Our simple smile and act of compassion/kindness may be all that will make the difference in the lives of our patients. Everything may seem kind of overwhelming right now; don't be discouraged. The Lord is with you, and very soon, He will make a way of escape for you, in the

215

name of Jesus. Amen! God has created you for a time like this and for a purpose. May He fulfill His purpose in your life, in the mighty name of Jesus. Amen!

The Lord did not promise that we will only see sunshine, but He promised to be with us. With Him on our sides, we are more than conquerors, in the name of Jesus. Amen! It is written: "*Yea, though I walk through the valley of the shadow of death, I will fear no evil; for You are with me; your rod and Your staff, they comfort me*" (Psalm 23:1&4). Living in any part of the world today could be a form of a "valley of the shadow of death." If it is not racism, it would be a misuse of power, poverty, crime or Fulani herdsmen/Boko Haram issues or the many other things threatening people's lives worldwide. David said he would not be afraid because God was with him. It is written: "*The LORD is my shepherd; I shall not want*" (Psalm 23:1; emphasis added). I pray that we will continue to enjoy the safety with our Lord and Savior. He is our shepherd. We don't need to worry about anything! He is in TOTAL CONTROL, in the mighty name of Jesus. Amen!

GOD WILL PROTECT YOU

You may be feeling like you are about to be thrown into a "fiery furnace." I pray that the God of Shadrach, Meshach and Abednego will protect you from any form of "Nebuchadnezzar," who may be angry at you, in the name of Jesus. Amen! The more you serve God, the more the enemy wages war against you and gives you more advance level trials. After you overcome one obstacle, you might have to face another challenging situation that may make you feel like you are about to be consumed. Fear not. The good Lord is with you, fighting your battles. He is able to hide and protect you. No matter how strong the storms of life may be, may we remain under the shadow of God. May He hide and protect us from ALL harms and dangers. May He stay in the "fire" with us and bring us out safely, in the mighty name of Jesus Amen (Daniel 3)!

It is written: *"Then Nebuchadnezzar was full of fury, and the expression on his face changed toward Shadrach, Meshach, and Abednego. He spoke and commanded that they heat the furnace seven times more than it was usually heated. And he commanded certain mighty men of valor who were in his army to bind Shadrach, Meshach, and Abednego, and cast them into the burning fiery furnace. Then these men were bound in their coats, their trousers, their turbans, and their other garments, and were cast into the midst of the burning fiery furnace. Therefore,*

217

because the king's command was urgent, and the furnace exceedingly hot, the flame of the fire killed those men who took up Shadrach, Meshach, and Abednego. And these three men, Shadrach, Meshach, and Abednego, fell down bound into the midst of the burning fiery furnace. Then King Nebuchadnezzar was astonished; and he rose in haste and spoke, saying to his counselors, "Did we not cast three men bound into the midst of the fire?" They answered and said to the king, "True, O king." "Look!" he answered, "I see four men loose, walking in the midst of the fire; and they are not hurt, and the form of the fourth is like the Son of God" (Daniel 3:19-25 NKJV). Hallelujah! What a mighty God we serve! As He was with the three Hebrew boys, so shall He be with you and surprise all the "Nebuchadnezzars" in your life, in the name of Jesus. Amen! It is human to worry, when we find ourselves, in the mist of trials, failures, tribulations and the uncertainties of this world. Let us invite Jesus and the host of heaven to surround and deliver us from ALL harms and dangers. When we are in any form of "fiery furnace," and anxiety, depression, diabetes, high blood pressure, cancer and other ill heath are looking for ways to come into our lives, I pray that the good Lord will stay with us, shield/protect us, in the mighty name of Jesus.

Song of Meditation "When the storms of Life Are Raging, Stand by Me" By: Charles Albert Tindley (1905)

1 When the storms of life are raging,

stand by me; (stand by me)

when the storms of life are raging,

stand by me. (stand by me)

When the world is tossing me

like a ship upon the sea,

thou who rulest wind and water,

stand by me. (stand by me)

2 In the midst of tribulation,

stand by me; (stand by me)

in the midst of tribulation,

stand by me. (stand by me)

When the hosts of hell assail,

and my strength begins to fail,

thou who never lost a battle,

stand by me. (stand by me)

3 In the midst of faults and failures,

stand by me; (stand by me)

in the midst of faults and failures,

stand by me. (stand by me)

When I've done the best I can,

and my friends misunderstand,

thou who knowest all about me,

stand by me. (stand by me)

4 In the midst of persecution,

stand by me; (stand by me)

in the midst of persecution,

stand by me. (stand by me)

When my foes in war array

undertake to stop my way,

thou who rescued Paul and Silas,

stand by me. (stand by me)

5 When I'm growing old and feeble,

stand by me; (stand by me)

when I'm growing old and feeble,

stand by me. (stand by me)

When my life becomes a burden,

and I'm nearing chilly Jordan,

O thou Lily of the Valley,

stand by me. (stand by me)

GOD WILL CALL YOU OUT OF THE "FIRE!"

Your present situation may be challenging and hopeless. I pray that your life's testimonies will be so great that the world will know that you serve a mighty and loving Savior who is able to save. Glory! I pray that many souls will be drawn to God because of what He is about to do in your life. You are about to be promoted, in the mighty name of Jesus. Amen! (Daniel 3:26-30).

The God of Daniel (Daniel 6) is with you. May God deliver you from the hands of those plotting evil against you. I pray that the world will not fool your helper, friend and loved ones into signing papers that will get you into trouble, in the name of Jesus. Amen! It is written: *"So these governors and satraps thronged before the king, and said thus to him: "King Darius, live forever! All the governors of the kingdom, the administrators and satraps, the counselors and advisors, have consulted together to establish a royal statute and to make a firm decree, that whoever petitions any god or man for thirty days, except you, O king, shall be cast into the den of lions. Now, O king, establish the decree and sign the writing, so that it cannot be changed, according to the law of the Medes and Persians, which does not alter." Therefore, King Darius signed the written decree"* (Daniel 6:6-9 NKJV). The king did not plan to hurt Daniel, and He did not even have a clue that the "royal statute" was a plan to get Daniel. May God help all of us be mindful of "fame" that will involve the destruction of souls. May God help us guard against those who may be interested in using our names to do evil, in the mighty name of Jesus.

I pray that God will deliver us from the hands of the wicked ones, in the name of Jesus. Amen! It is written: *"Now when Daniel knew that the writing was signed, he went home. And in his upper room, with his windows open toward Jerusalem, he knelt down on his knees three times that day, and prayed and gave thanks before his God, as was his custom since early days. Then these men assembled and found Daniel praying and making supplication before his God. And they went before the king, and spoke concerning the king's decree: "Have you not signed a decree that every man who petitions any god or man within thirty days, except you, O king, shall be cast into the den of lions?" The king answered and said, "The thing is true, according to the law of the Medes and Persians, which does not alter." So they answered and said before the king, "That Daniel, who is one of the captives from*

223

Judah, does not show due regard for you, O king, or for the decree that you have signed, but makes his petition three times a day" *And the king, when he heard these words, was greatly displeased with himself, and set his heart on Daniel to deliver him; and he labored till the going down of the sun to deliver him. Then these men approached the king, and said to the king, "know, O king, that it is the law of the Medes and Persians that no decree or statute which the king establishes may be changed." So, the king gave the command, and they brought Daniel and cast him into the den of lions. But the king spoke, saying to Daniel, "Your God, whom you serve continually, He will deliver you." Then a stone was brought and laid on the mouth of the den, and the king sealed it with his own signet ring and with the signets of his lords, that the purpose concerning Daniel might not be changed"* (Daniel 6:10-17 NKJV). It is not over with you, except when God says so. Has someone signed your termination letter? Hold on to God. Your spouse just handed you a divorce paper? Hold on to God. I pray that any form of document signed to work against you will not have power over you. Let them sign the "papers"; you will not be consumed, and God will deliver you, in the mighty name of Jesus. Amen!

God will turn your "lions" into vegetarians and will not permit them to hurt you, in the name of Jesus. Amen! It is written: *"Now the king went to his palace and spent the night fasting; and no musicians were brought before him. Also, his sleep went from him. Then the king arose very early in the morning and went in haste*

224

to the den of lions. And when he came to the den, he cried out with a lamenting voice to Daniel. The king spoke, saying to Daniel, "Daniel, servant of the living God, has your God, whom you serve continually, been able to deliver you from the lions?" Then Daniel said to the king, "O king, live forever! My God sent His angel and shut the lions' mouths, so that they have not hurt me, because I was found innocent before Him; and also, O king, I have done no wrong before you." Now the king was exceedingly glad for him, and commanded that they should take Daniel up out of the den. So, Daniel was taken up out of the den, and no injury whatever was found on him, because he believed in his God" (Daniel 6:18-23 NKJV). You are coming out safe and sound from WHATEVER is challenging you, in the mighty name of Jesus. Amen!

YOU WILL NOT BE PUT TO SHAME

I t is written: *"And the king gave the command, and they brought those men who had accused Daniel, and they cast them into the den of lions—them, their children, and their wives; and the lions overpowered them, and broke all their bones in pieces before they ever came to the bottom of the den. Then King Darius wrote: To all peoples, nations, and languages that dwell in all the earth: Peace be multiplied to you. I make a decree that in every dominion of my kingdom men must tremble and fear before the God of Daniel. For He is the living God, and steadfast forever; His kingdom is the one which shall not be destroyed, And His dominion shall endure to the end. He delivers and rescues, And He works signs and wonders in heaven and on earth, who has delivered Daniel from the power of the lions. So, this Daniel prospered in the reign of Darius and in the reign of Cyrus the Persian"* (Daniel 6:24-28 NKJV). We cannot prevent people from plotting evil. I pray that your enemies will fall into the traps they have set for you, and whoever gathers against you will fall for your sake, in the name of Jesus. Amen!

Are you having a "Red Sea moment," and are you wondering how you will cross over to safety? The God of Israel who parted the Red Sea is still alive and more than able to see you through, in the name of Jesus. He will part the "Red Sea" for you and your loved ones. God will close the "waters" up on your enemies who are planning to destroy you, in the name of Jesus (Exodus 14). Is there any form of "Goliath" underestimating what God can do for you and in you? The God of David will provide the "anointed stone," directed by the "divine GPS" that will land perfectly on your "Goliath's" head and pull him down, in the mighty name of Jesus. Amen (1 Samuel 17)!

Are you concerned about what is going to become of you? Jehovah-Jireh has promised that He will supply ALL (not some of them but ALL) of your needs according to His riches in glory by Christ Jesus (Philippians 4:19). Do not forget His promise that SURELY (not maybe), goodness and mercy shall follow you, ALL the days of your life (Psalm 23:6). Hallelujah! Your daily bread will be provided, in the name of Jesus. It is written: "*I have been young, and now am old; Yet I have not seen the righteous forsaken, nor his descendants begging bread*" (Psalm 37:25). Amen! The good and merciful Father will NEVER leave nor forsake you. God promised that you and all yours will NEVER beg for bread, in the name of Jesus. God will prepare a table before you, in the presence of your enemies; He will anoint your head with oil, and your cup is about to run over, in the name of Jesus. Amen! His goodness and mercy will always be your portion. (Psalm 23:5-6). So, shall it be, in the mighty name of Jesus. Amen!

YOU SHALL BE COMFORTED!

Are you barren, trusting God for the fruit of the womb? The God who answered Hannah's prayer will answer your prayer, and you will soon testify of His goodness. Your "Samuel" is about to be delivered, in the mighty name of Jesus. Amen! Is your "barrenness" in the form of joblessness, lack of productivity in your business or inability to pass that exam yet? Is it a challenging marriage, a troublesome or disobedient child? Is it trouble with in-laws, family members or the unfriendly friends? Are your "Peninnahs" teasing you all the time? Maybe you don't even have "Elkanah" to comfort you. You are so lonely, frustrated and have no one to comfort you. The Lord says: *"Come to Me, all you who labor and are heavy laden, and I will give you rest. Take My yoke upon you and learn from Me, for I am gentle and lowly in heart, and you will find rest for your soul* (Matthew 11:28). Don't give up. It is written: *"For His anger is but for a moment, His favor is for life; Weeping may endure for a night, but joy comes in the morning"* (Psalm 30:5 NKJV). I pray that God will wipe your tears away, in the name of Jesus. Amen! It's "Friday," my darling brother/sister, "Sunday" is coming, and God will call all that is dead in you back to life, in the name of Jesus. It is written: *"And seeing the multitudes, He went up on a mountain, and when He was seated His disciples came to Him. Then He opened His mouth and taught them, saying: "Blessed are the poor in spirit, for theirs is the kingdom of heaven. Blessed are those who mourn, for they shall be comforted. Blessed are the meek, for they shall inherit the [a]earth. Blessed are those who hunger and thirst for righteousness, for they shall be filled. Blessed are the merciful, for they shall obtain mercy"* (Matthew 5:1-7 NKJV). The Lord is with you, leading and guiding you through the "valley." You are going to come out in peace, joy and sound health, in the name of Jesus. Amen!

Song of Meditation "We Shall Walk Through the Valley in Peace" By A. L. Hatter

WE ARE ALMOST HOME

Whatever the situation, darling child of God, anxiety/depression will not solve the problem; it will ONLY add to it. May God grant you the grace to cast your cares upon Him and to remember daily that He cares and loves you dearly. You have come this far by His grace. He has been your guide and shield; you are not going to give up, by the grace of God. Signs of the end times are everywhere; we are almost home. Be reminded that it won't be long before our Savior will come to take us home with Him. Whatever we may be going through here on earth is just a stepping stone, and this troubled world is not our final home. The good news, my brother/sister in the Lord, is that there is a home, a crown, robe and ALL the "goodies" up in that kingdom.

We are going to lay everything down and be reunited with our Savior and our loved ones, in the name of Jesus. Oh, what a happy day! We are going to rejoice in our Lord EVERY DAY. Glory, Hallelujah! Until then, let us continue to sing of the wondrous love of Jesus; let us sing about His mercy and His grace! My brother/sister, I tell you, when we all get to heaven and see Jesus, we will sing and shout for victory. There will be no more pain, no oppression and no plague. There will be no need to be afraid. Praise God! Until then, darling brother/sister in the Lord, I pray that our hearts will NEVER stop singing God's praises. May the good Lord grant us the grace to hold the fort until He comes, in the mighty name of Jesus. Amen!

Song of Meditation "Until Then" By Ray Price (1960)

Song of Meditation "Hold the Fort" By Philip P. Bliss (1870)

1. Ho, my comrades, see the signal, waving in the sky!
Reinforcements now appearing, victory is nigh.
Refrain
"Hold the fort, for I am coming,"
Jesus signals still; Wave the answer back to heaven,
"By Thy grace we will."

2. See the mighty host advancing, Satan leading on;
Mighty ones around us falling, courage almost gone!

3. See the glorious banner waving! Hear the trumpet blow!
In our Leader's Name we triumph over every foe.

4. Fierce and long the battle rages, but our help is near;
Onward comes our great Commander, cheer, my comrades,
cheer!

DIVINE IMMUNIZATION

In the medical world, when a child is born, the Centers for Disease Control and Prevention (CDC), recommends all sorts of immunizations for babies into adulthood to prevent illnesses. Moreover, there is something called a routine checkup to catch any form of disease development early. This helps patients to get help on time, and lives have been saved through these preventative medicines. I have good news for you. There are prophylactic measures in the Bible to protect us from trouble and the plans of the enemy as well! Whether the enemy likes it or not, we are bound for the promised land. It is written: *"Finally, my brethren, be strong in the Lord and in the power of His might. **Put on the whole armor of God** that you may be able to stand against the wiles of the devil. For we do not wrestle against flesh and blood, but against principalities, against powers, against the rulers of the darkness of this age, against spiritual hosts of wickedness in the heavenly places. Therefore, take up the whole armor of God that you may be able to withstand in the evil day, and having done all, to stand. Stand therefore, having girded your waist with truth, having put on the breastplate of righteousness, and having shod your feet with the preparation of the gospel of peace; above all, taking the shield of faith with which, you will be able to quench all the fiery darts of the wicked one. And take the helmet of salvation, and the sword of the Spirit, which is the word* *of God; praying always with all prayer and supplication in the Spirit, being watchful to this end with all perseverance and supplication for all the saints"* (Ephesians 6:10-18 NKJV; emphasis added). Compliance with the above instructions will protect us from UNNECESSARY trouble. May we get our spiritual "IMMUNIZATION" today from the Christ Deliverance Center (our spiritual CDC). It is done remotely, in the comfort of our homes. All we need to do is submit our EVERYTHING to God, accepting Him as our Lord and Savior and soaking ourselves in His word on a daily basis. May we remain protected with the precious blood, shed on Calvary, in the mighty name of Jesus. Amen!

THE CHURCH YOU ATTEND CAN MAKE OR BREAK YOU

The Lord wants us to fellowship together. It is written: *"Not forsaking the assembling of ourselves together, as is the manner of some, but exhorting one another, and so much the more as you see the day approaching"* (Hebrews 10:25 NKJV). Church can serve as a supportive community. Notwithstanding, beware of the type of churches you go to and take time to study the word yourself. **DO NOT** depend on your pastor's teachings **alone.** Search the scriptures and see that the teachings are true. Some pastors will ask their members to eat grass like animals. Some will take advantage of them in different ways that are so nasty, and I don't even want to write about it. There are many social gatherings and clubhouses, people call "church," these days. Opening a church could be a very "lucrative business." One must be **EXTREMELY** careful. The church you attend can make or break you.

Dear child of God, you really need to know that if the "temperature" of the church you attend is cool and comfortable for the enemy, it could be very dangerous and challenging for you to be all that God wants you to be. You are likely to have "spiritual hypothermia." You might become spiritually "malnourished" or be prone to "spiritual retardation/failure to thrive" if you are not well nourished, not "fed" adequately, or you belong to that church where all you do is "sowing seeds" (spiritual robbery on the part

234

of the so-called pastors). The pastor is getting richer, while the church members are getting poorer. Beware of churches where Malachi 3:10 is being used to rob God's children, who are striving not to "rob" God and want to be faithful in their giving. It is written: *"Bring all the tithes into the storehouse, that there may be food in My house, and try me now in this," Says the LORD of hosts, "If I will not open for you the windows of heaven and pour out for you such blessing that there will not be room enough to receive it"* (Malachi 3:10 NKJV). It is important to give that 10% of our income and offerings as the Lord instructed. In addition, we are to give our offerings as the spirit leads. To whom much is given, much is expected. No one should be forced to do what he/she cannot afford.

Growing up, we used to have poultry and a little garden in our backyard where our mother planted vegetables. This idea really helped because of the unannounced visitors we often had due to the nature of my father's job (a pastor). The mega salary of my father couldn't cover the expenses of entertaining visitors the way we did. The poultry and the little garden helped. When cleaning and cutting the chicken, my mother paid SPECIAL attention to the gall bladder. Until she was able to remove this small part of the chicken, she was unsure if the soup would be possible. She educated us, telling us that if the gall bladder should burst and spill on the other parts of the chicken, we won't be able to eat it because it would taste bitter. She used to attribute this analogy to tithe paying. The long and short of my story is: For you to really enjoy any form of "chicken" (income), kindly take that small portion (gallbladder/tithe) out, please. There is nothing wrong with being very generous and giving more than the tithe and offering to propagate the work of God. What is wrong is when a pastor forces you to do more than you are able to do. Don't become a victim of robbery, all in the name of God. It is written: *"But this I say: He who sows sparingly will also reap sparingly, and he who sows bountifully will also reap bountifully. So let each one give as he purposes in his heart, not grudgingly or of necessity; for God loves a cheerful giver"* (2 Corinthians 9:6-7 NKJV). I come against any form of devourer in your life, in the name of Jesus. Amen!

Are you where prosperity preaching has replaced sermons that will point you to heaven and remind you that Jesus is coming very soon? Are the leaders who are supposed to be sowing seeds of faith, repentance and courage in you, the ones requesting that you "sow seeds" (money), and it seems like campaigns for money or pocket filling has replaced altar calls. Lord have mercy! I pray that God will take off WHATEVER they might have used to charm you. May God show you the light and get you out of "Babylon," in the mighty name of Jesus. Amen!

You can imagine spiritual leaders allowing the love of money, position in society, fame and chieftaincy titles be the determining factors of how they relate to their members and how their church officials are elected. While some churches are busy getting souls ready for the Lord, some are into prosperity preaching. Oh, the judgment day is coming; what an awful day it will be! Glory be to God that the ticket to heaven is not something that can be bought with money. Jesus has paid it ALL with His PRECIOUS blood on the cross of Calvary. Hallelujah! Where will those who are unable to sow seeds be, if not for God and the death of Jesus on Calvary? Just imagine what could have happened to the "poor." Some of these false prophets will be using psychology on their members, stating that they saw a "vision." They will be talking about the challenges they know the member is going through; they will start speaking in MEMORIZED language and call it "speaking in tongues." They take the meekness of their members for weakness. Some of the ones I have encountered say the same language all the time because it is memorized. It is not from God.

Don't get me wrong, please. I believe in speaking in tongues. It is written: *"And these signs will follow those who believe: In My name they will cast out demons; they will speak with new tongues"* (Mark 16:17 NKJV). Furthermore, the Bible says: *"Pursue love, and desire spiritual gifts, but especially that you may prophesy. For he who speaks in a tongue does not speak to men but to God, for no one understands him; however, in the spirit he speaks mysteries. But he who prophesies speaks edification and exhortation and comfort to men. He who speaks in a tongue edifies himself, but he who prophesies edifies the church. I wish you all spoke with tongues, but even more that you prophesied; for he who prophesies is greater than he who speaks with tongues, unless indeed he interprets, that the church may receive edification"* (1 Corinthians 14:1-5 NKJV).

In addition, it is written: *"But now, brethren, if I come to you speaking with tongues, what shall I profit you unless I speak to you either by revelation, by knowledge, by prophesying, or by teaching? Even things without life, whether flute or harp, when they make a sound, unless they make a distinction in the sounds, how will it be known what is piped or played? For if the trumpet makes an uncertain sound, who will prepare for battle? So likewise, you, unless you utter by the tongue words easy to understand, how will it be known what is spoken? For you will be speaking into the air. There are, it may be, so many kinds of languages in the world, and none of them is without significance. Therefore, if I do not know the meaning of the language, I shall be a foreigner to him who speaks, and he who speaks will be a foreigner to me. Even so you, since you are zealous for spiritual gifts, let it be for the edification of the church that you seek to excel"* (1 Corinthians 14:6-12 NKJV).

For more understanding, it is written: *"Therefore, let him who speaks in a tongue pray that he may interpret. For if I pray in a tongue, my spirit prays, but my understanding is unfruitful. What is the conclusion then? I will pray with the spirit, and I will also pray with the understanding. I will sing with the spirit, and I will also sing with the understanding. Otherwise, if you bless with the spirit, how will he who occupies the place of the uninformed say "Amen" at your giving of thanks, since he does not understand what you say? For you indeed give thanks well, but the other is not edified. I thank my God I speak with tongues more than you all; yet in the church I would rather speak five words with my understanding, that I may teach others also, than ten thousand words in a tongue"* (1 Corinthians 13:19 NKJV).

We have to be very careful. Many souls are dying because of the high standards and expectations of some pastors that are unrealistic. Some members may stop going to church if they are unable to meet the standard set for them. They may be feeling ashamed or guilty. As simple as it sounds, these may lead to depression, feelings of inadequacy and other negative feelings, including members isolating themselves or withdrawing completely. Lord have mercy! We have been warned against false prophets. It is written: *"For the time will come when they will not endure sound doctrine, but according to their own desires, because they have itching ears, they will heap up for themselves teachers; and they will turn their ears away from the truth, and be turned aside to fables"* (2 Timothy 4:3-4 NKJV). *"For false Christ and false prophets will rise and show great signs and wonders to deceive, if possible, even the elect"* (Matthew 24:24 NKJV). May God help us all not to be victims, in the mighty name of Jesus. Amen!

"Thus says the LORD of hosts: "Do not listen to the words of the prophets who prophesy to you.

They make you worthless; They speak a vision of their own heart, not from the mouth of the LORD. They continually say to those who despise Me, 'the LORD has said, "you shall have peace"'; And to everyone who walks according to the dictates of his own heart, they say,

'No evil shall come upon you.'" For who has stood in the counsel of the LORD, and has perceived and heard His word? Who has marked His word and heard it?" (Jeremiah 23:16-18 NKJV).

I have news for these prophets. It is written: *"My hand will be against the prophets who envision futility and who divine lies; they shall not be in the assembly of My people, nor be written in the record of the house of Israel, nor shall they enter into the land of Israel. Then you shall know that I am the Lord GOD"* (Ezekiel 13:9 NKJV). In case you don't know, it is written: *"A false witness will not go unpunished, and he who speaks lies will not escape"* (Proverbs 19:5 NKJV).

Darling brother/sister, it is written: *"Therefore, take heed to yourselves and to all the flock, among which the Holy Spirit has made you overseers, to shepherd the church of God which He purchased with His own blood. For I know this, that after my departure savage wolves will come in among you, not sparing the flock. Also, from among yourselves men will rise up, speaking perverse things, to draw away the disciples after themselves"* (Acts 20:28-30 NKJV). May our foundation be firm in the Lord,

240

and may we be rooted deep, in God's words, in the mighty name of Jesus. Amen!

If you decide to remain in this type of church, you will soon be "diagnosed" with spiritual "kwashiorkor," which could predispose you to frequent spiritual attacks (spiritual infections), spiritual growth retardation, thin prayer line (thin hair), a "big belly" full of lies due to, lack of adequate nourishment of God's words and affirmation of whom you are in Christ. Instead of growing stronger in the Lord, one may end up with low self-esteem that may eventually lead to UNNECESSARY anxiety, depression and if care is not taken, may lead to suicide. Dear child of God, kindly take off the "veil/makeup" and go to where you will be nurtured before it is too late. You have to get out of "BABYLON," please.

Furthermore, to those pastors and officials in the church who think having the opportunity to mount the pulpit or having access to the microphone is a chance to verbally abuse that member you have been looking for the opportunity to "lash" with words—God sees your heart. Our words are to heal and not for destruction. I encourage that we remember these Bible verses before speaking: *"You have tested my heart; You have visited me in the night; You have tried me and have found nothing; I have purposed that my mouth shall not transgress"* (Psalm 17:3 NKJV).

"For He who would love life and see good days, let him refrain his tongue from evil,

And his lips from speaking deceit" (1 Peter 3:10 NKJV).

"Let no corrupt word proceed out of your mouth, but what is good for necessary edification, that it may impart grace to the hearers" (Ephesians 4:29).

"Set a guard, O LORD, over my mouth; Keep watch over the door of my lips" (Psalm 141:3 NKJV). As from today, may our prayer be Father, please: *"Let the words of my mouth and the meditation of my heart be acceptable in Your sight, O Lord, my strength and my Redeemer"* (Psalm 19:14 NKJV). Amen!

This message is for all of us. It is written: *"Therefore, beloved, looking forward to these things, be diligent to be found by Him in peace, without spot and blameless; and consider that the longsuffering of our Lord is salvation—as also our beloved brother Paul, according to the wisdom given to him, has written to you, as also in all his epistles, speaking in them of these things, in which are some things hard to understand, which untaught and unstable people twist to their own destruction, as they do also the rest of the Scriptures. You therefore, beloved, since you know this beforehand, beware lest you also fall from your own steadfastness, being led away with the error of the wicked; but grow in the grace and knowledge of our Lord and Savior Jesus Christ. To Him be the glory both now and forever. Amen"* (2 Peter 3:14-18 NKJV).

Moreover, I will encourage that we belong to the right fellowship, not a "social gathering" that is covering up under the "umbrella" of church. Go to where people fellowship and pray in truth and spirit, where they plead the blood of Jesus and call on His holy name with the authority given by God Himself, not the power they have received from other gods. It is written: *"That at the name of Jesus every knee should bow, of those in heaven, and of those on earth, and of those under the earth"* (Philippians 2:10 NKJV). May God direct you to a church that is very "HOT" and uncomfortable for the enemy to stay. When you join them, do not quench the "fire" either, but add to the "hotness." Light and darkness can NEVER stay together. When light enters into a dark room, darkness has to disappear fast. I speak light into your life today, in the name of Jesus. May you shine so bright to the point that any form of "darkness" will not be able to stand your presence, in the name of Jesus. Cover you with the blood of Jesus and pray that God will build the wall of fire around you and make you UNTOUCHABLE, in the name of Jesus. Amen! It is written: *"Now the blood shall be a sign for you on the houses where you are. And when I see the blood, I will pass over you; and the plague shall not be on you to destroy you when I strike the land of Egypt"* (Exodus 12:13 NKJV). When the evil angels or any form of plaque see the mark of the blood of Jesus over your "doorpost," they have to pass, and God will redirect the arrows of the enemies, in the name of Jesus. He will guide and protect you. Jesus shed His blood on Calvary for you and me to be saved. The BLOOD will NEVER lose its power, in the mighty name of Jesus. Amen!

Song of Meditation "What Can Wash Away My Sin?" By
Robert Lowry (1876)

1. What can wash away my sin?

Nothing but the blood of Jesus;

What can make me whole again?

Nothing but the blood of Jesus.

Refrain

Oh! precious is the flow

That makes me white as snow;

No other fount I know,

Nothing but the blood of Jesus.

2. For my pardon, this I see,

Nothing but the blood of Jesus;

For my cleansing this my plea,

Nothing but the blood of Jesus.

3. Nothing can for sin atone,

Nothing but the blood of Jesus;

Naught of good that I have done,

Nothing but the blood of Jesus.

4. This is all my hope and peace,

Nothing but the blood of Jesus;

This is all my righteousness,

Nothing but the blood of Jesus.

5. Now by this I'll overcome—
Nothing but the blood of Jesus;
Now by this I'll reach my home—
Nothing but the blood of Jesus.

6. Glory! Glory! This I sing—
Nothing but the blood of Jesus,
All my praise for this I bring—
Nothing but the blood of Jesus.

FALL IN LOVE WITH THE BIBLE

Take off the "makeup/veil" and reject the spirits of negativity, anxiety, depression, hopelessness, suicidal or homicide ideations in your life that are making you run to the false prophets. You don't need an intermediary. You don't have to wait in line. You need Jesus and your Bible. We are to continually remind ourselves of God's promises to us, meditate on them and put what we read into practice. May God help us to "fall in love" with our Bibles, the "holy message shining," as we travel along the "wilderness journey." May the "light" guide us through the narrow ways of life. May it equip us to discern false prophets and their teachings. May it prosper us, grant us "good success" and prepare us for the second coming of our Savior, Redeemer and Friend, in the mighty name of Jesus. Amen!

Song of Meditation "Give Me the Bible" By Priscilla J. Owens

1. Give me the Bible, star of gladness gleaming,
To cheer the wand'rer lone and tempest tossed;
No storm can hide that peaceful radiance beaming,
Since Jesus came to seek and save the lost.

Chorus
Give me the Bible, Holy message shining,
Thy light shall guide me in the narrow way.
Precept and promise, law and love combining,
Till night shall vanish in eternal day.

2. Give me the Bible, star of gladness gleaming,
To cheer the wand'rer lone and tempest tossed;
No storm can hide that radiance peaceful beaming,
Since Jesus came to seek and save the lost.

3. Give me the Bible, when my heart is broken,
When sin and grief have filled my soul with fear;
Give me the precious words by Jesus spoken,
Hold up faith's lamp to show my Savior near.

MISUNDERSTOOD AND MISDIAGNOSED

There is a limit to how long we can cover things up. The veil/makeup may fail us one day. The "fitted veil" may start to become very loose and unable to cover the whole face. Unfortunately, some people may not take the time necessary to really get to know us. They may start to give us all sorts of names and diagnoses based on the uncovered part of the face and the negative reports they might have received about us. They may draw the conclusion that you must really have issues because of the reports people have given. This may cut people off from you, and you may be feeling isolated. You may lose some friends who are dear to you. Don't be disappointed to find out that they never took you seriously in the first place. You don't need to worry; ignore the lies. Yes, we all have issues. Some of your issues could be loving to a fault, assuming everyone believes in the "golden rule," and not knowing how to say no. It is time to approach God's throne of grace and allow Him to fix your "issue/s." Take off the veil/makeup; don't let anyone misdiagnose or misunderstand you. Be real, be you and start loving yourself because you are an AMAZING son/daughter of God. He loves you dearly. He died for you.

I am from Nigeria, West Africa, from the Yoruba tribe, where the naming ceremony is meaningful and very important. In most of the tribes in Nigeria, we don't just pick a name randomly for our children. We consider many things. I won't be able to mention everything, but I will cite a few examples. The circumstances surrounding the birth of the child, for instance; if the parents received promotion/blessings, around the time the child was born, the child's name might be; Olugbenga, Oluyemisi, Oluponmile and many more. Nigerians believe that names have power and it will follow the child forever. So, they give meaningful names to their children. The way the child presents at birth or the day of the week the child is born, may also determine the name. For example, a child who presents with legs first will be called "Ige"; the child with the cord around the neck is called "Aina" and many more. According to the culture, uncles, aunties, grandmas or grandpas who want to give that child a name will give money or a gift. Sometimes, the child may not know all the names he or she has. When the child visits family members, the child may be called a name he or she has never heard before, but the child will know that the family member might have given him/her the name during the naming ceremony.

This book is not about the naming ceremony in Nigeria. The point I want to make is that if you were not present during my naming ceremony, and you did not give my parents money for naming, I can say with all due respect that you have no right to call me ANY name that is not mine, most especially, the negative ones. If you have decided to do so anyway, I have the right to the names I want to respond to. When I was in high school, we had some seniors who were bullies. One day, my classmates and I were playing in

249

the front of the hostel, and a senior called out, "You animals, come here." My friends were terrified. To avoid punishment, they decided to answer. I did not get up from my spot. I continued with what I was doing. The senior got so angry, and she reported me to some of her friends, and they all came for me. I was not afraid. She asked me, "Why didn't you answer when I called you?" I said, "She did not call me." Respectfully, I told her I did not hear my name. The anger in her and her friends increased. She said, "Do you think you are better than the ones who answered or do you think you have two heads?" I told her they probably answered to their names. They (the seniors) all decided to punish me. Politely, I said, "I will not do the punishment unless we go to the principal and state our cases." They knew they were wrong, so they left me and released my friends as well.

Some people may not call you negative names, but they will try to change your name because it sounds different from what they are used to. They may start by saying, "Your name is difficult for me to pronounce. Can I call you Jane, Tom or Mike?" No sir/ma'am! My name is **BOSEDE**. If I can learn to pronounce your own name, I see no reason why you shouldn't be able to pronounce mine. It's all about love, acceptance and respect. Brother/sister, you don't have to be a Nigerian to have this principle. You may not understand the meaning of your name, and your culture may not have anything called a naming ceremony. No matter your culture, your tribe, skin color, social or economic status, we are all children of God. It is written: "*I will be a Father*

250

to you, and you shall be My sons and daughters, says the LORD Almighty" (2 Corinthians 6:18 NKJV). Let me just remind you of some of the names our heavenly Father has for His children, including you:

REDEEMED: *"I have blotted out, like a thick cloud, your transgressions, and like a cloud, your sins. Return to Me, for I have redeemed you"* (Isaiah 44:22 NKJV. *"In Him we have redemption through His blood, the forgiveness of sins, according to the riches of His grace"* (Ephesians 1:7 NKJV).

BELOVED and ELECT: *"Therefore, as the elect of God, holy and beloved, put on tender mercies, kindness, humility, meekness, longsuffering"* (Colossians 3:12 NKJV).

CHOSEN, ROYAL PRIESTHOOD, HOLY NATION and GOD'S SPECIAL PEOPLE: *"But you are a chosen generation, a royal priesthood, a holy nation, His own special people, that you may proclaim the praises of Him who called you out of darkness into His marvelous light"* (1 Peter 2:9 NKJV).

PRECIOUS: *"Since you were precious in my sight, you have been honored, and I have loved you; Therefore, I will give men for you, and people for your life"* (Isaiah 43:4 NKJV).

SPECIAL TREASURE *"For you are a holy people to the LORD your God; the LORD your God has chosen you to be a people for Himself, a special treasure above all the peoples on the face of the earth"* (Deuteronomy 7:6 NKJV).

A NEW CREATION: *"Therefore, if anyone is in Christ, he is a new creation; old things have passed away; behold, all things have become new"* (2 Corinthians 5:17 NKJV).

I don't know the names you have been answering to. It is never too late to remind those who might have forgotten your name and are trying to give you names that are not yours that the Lord has called you by name and that you are prince/princess of the Most High God. Kindly do the NECESSARY change of name, as needed. You are a child of God. I pray that NOTHING and NO ONE will tarnish your name, in the mighty name of Jesus. Amen! Remain blessed, precious child of God.

Song of Meditation "Take the Name of Jesus With You" By Lydia Baxter (1870)

1. Take the name of Jesus with you,

Child of sorrow and of woe.

It will joy and comfort give you,

Take it then where'er you go.

Refrain

Precious name, O how sweet!

Hope of earth and joy of heaven;

Precious name, O how sweet!

Hope of earth and joy of heaven.

2. Take the name of Jesus ever

As protection ev'rywhere.

If temptations 'round you gather,

Breathe that holy name in prayer.

3. At the name of Jesus bowing,

When in heaven we shall meet,

King of kings, we'll gladly crown him

When our journey is complete.

INNOCENT MISTAKES

In our spiritual journey, we make some "innocent mistakes" that sometimes get us into serious troubles. There are many bumps, thorns, pits, "lion's dens," "fiery furnaces" and many other challenges on the way. Moreover, our Creator sometimes allows some things to happen to us for purification so that when He is done working with us, we can come out shining like gold, and His name will be glorified. We are not alone. There are some examples in the Bible about innocent mistakes made and how we can fall into the same trap.

Have You Told People Your Dreams of Greatness?

Sometimes, we indirectly invite trouble into our lives by telling the "wrong people" about our plans, blessings, goals in life or our dreams. Many times, we talk too much. There is an adage that says: "A pregnant woman does not need any announcement/testimony about her pregnancy; it will be known at the appointed time." We learned that Joseph's challenges started when he told his brothers his plans, and they became jealous of him. It is written: *"Now Joseph had a dream, and he told it to his brothers; and they hated him even more. So, he said to them, "please hear this dream which I have dreamed: There we were, binding sheaves in the field. Then behold, my sheaf arose and also stood upright; and indeed, your sheaves stood all around and bowed down to my sheaf. And his brothers said to him, "Shall you indeed reign over us? Or shall you indeed have dominion over us?" So, they hated him even more for his dreams and for his words. Then he dreamed still another dream and told it to his brothers, and said, "Look, I have dreamed another dream. And this time, the sun, the moon, and the eleven stars bowed down to me." So, he told it to his father and his brothers; and his father rebuked him and said to him, "What is this dream that you have dreamed? Shall your mother and I and your brothers indeed come to bow down to the earth before you"* (Genesis 37:5-10 NKJV).

Dear brother "Joseph" and sister "Josephine," kindly KEEP YOUR DREAMS TO YOURSELF, PLEASE! It is written: *"Wise people store up knowledge, but the mouth of the foolish is near destruction. In the multitude of words sin is not lacking, but he who restrains his lips is wise. The tongue of the righteous is choice silver; The heart of the wicked is worth little. The lips of the righteous feed many, but fools die for lack of wisdom"* (Proverbs 10:14, 19-21 NKJV). May God grant us the grace to know when to talk and when to keep quiet, in the mighty name of Jesus. Amen!

Have the "Wise Men" In Your Life Broadcasted Your Shining Star to the "Wrong King"

The wise men from the east almost got Jesus and His parents in trouble, indirectly and innocently. It is written: *"Now after Jesus was born in Bethlehem of Judea in the days of Herod the king, behold, wise men from the east came to Jerusalem, saying, "Where is He who has been born King of the Jews?* ***For we have seen His star in the east and have come to worship Him.*** *" When Herod the king heard this, he was troubled, and all Jerusalem with him. And when he had gathered all the chief priests and scribes of the people together, he inquired of them where the Christ was to be born"* (Matthew 2:1-4 NKJV; emphasis added). Not everyone seeking your address or your whereabouts means well. Be careful! May we not seek the way from the kidnapers or anyone with evil intention, who will lead us to a "dead end," in the mighty name of Jesus. Amen!

I pray that God will help the "wise men" in our lives (e.g., parents, uncles, aunties, siblings) not to expose us to unnecessary danger and for our church members/prayer partners, to mind how they share whatever we might have confided in them that is not meant for the consumption of others, most especially during the time they give PRAYER POINTS AND TESTIMONIES. May they not turn whatever we might have shared with them into "spiritual gossip." They may start by saying, "We thank God on behalf of sister/brother so and so for God's blessings of ... Kindly pray for brother/sister..." and the "gossip" will start. Did they ask you to testify or present their issues to the church? It is possible to make the testimonies/prayer requests anonymous. People don't need the full details, and God already knows before we say anything. Don't turn testimony/prayer time to "CNN," "FOX" or any other news stations, please. The embarrassments that may come out of these may make people leave the church. May God help us maintain confidentiality and learn to respect people's privacy, in the name of Jesus. Amen!

Prayer

God of Joseph, I thank you for the life of your child reading this book now. If your child has told his/her dream of greatness to those who will want to harm him or her, I pray that you provide brother "Reuben" and "Judah," who will protect your child from being killed. Deliver this your child from the hands of the enemy of progress. May the "Wise Men" in his/her life not seek direction regarding your child from any form of "King Herod." Remove your child from the pit they might have put him/her, in the name of Jesus. No matter who must have heard about his/her dream, erase it from their memory. Kindly perfect your will and lead your child safely to his/her land of greatness, in the mighty name of Jesus. Amen!

IS YOUR STAR TOO BRIGHT FOR THE ENEMY?

S omehow, some people have the power to see that someone has a very bright future. Some will put it this way: The star of that child is very bright. This child may start having problems from the moment his or her bright star is noticed. Someone once told me that I have a very bright "star." If God has blessed you with a very bright "star" or an AMAZING spirit, He will SURELY guide and protect you from the destiny changers. You may have to go from the pit to the prison but rest assured—you will one day make it to the PALACE by the grace of God. Amen! He did it for Joseph. He protected baby Jesus from the jealous King Herod. I pray that the "GPS" of the "Herods" in your life will malfunction, and they won't be able to locate you, in the name of Jesus. Nothing will deem your bright and shining "star." You will be all that God has created you to be, in the mighty name of Jesus. Amen!

It is written: *"Then Herod, when he had secretly called the wise men, determined from them what time the star appeared. And he sent them to Bethlehem and said, "Go and search carefully for the young Child, and when you have found Him, **BRING BACK WORD TO ME, THAT I MAY COME AND WORSHIP HIM ALSO"*** (Matthew 2:7-8 NKJV; emphasis added). Very cunny! Sounds nice but very dangerous. May God deliver us from the hands of people with "sugar-coated" mouths, the unfriendly friends and the wolves in sheep cloth. It is written: *"His words are as smooth as butter, but in his heart is war. His words are as soothing as lotion, but underneath are daggers"* (Psalm 55:21 NLT). *"Smooth words may hide a wicked heart, just as a pretty glaze covers a clay pot. People may cover their hatred with pleasant words, but they're deceiving you. They pretend to be kind, at the same time, be very careful but don't believe them. Their hearts are full of many evils"* (Proverbs 26:23-25 NLT). Lord have mercy! Let me quickly say that you may be wearing your "veil/makeup," trying to cover things up, but you will be surprised that there are some people with the "investigative spirit" or "magnifying/telescopic eyes" who are interested in what is going on in your life. If they can't see through your makeup/veil, they might try to sweet talk you, and you may be the one to uncover everything by what you tell them. We try to discourage "close-ended" communication, but this is what is needed when dealing with the ones with these "inquisitive spirits." May God deliver us and shield us from any form of "investigative spirit" and the unfriendly friends, in the mighty name of Jesus. Amen!

IT'S TIME TO REROUTE

For those of us who are familiar with the Global Positioning System (GPS), the word rerouting may not be strange to us. When we make a wrong turn, miss our way or where there is traffic or any form of delay, the GPS may reroute to another direction to avoid these problems. It's so amazing how much Siri knows! The star was the GPS that directed the Wise Men, and they were divinely warned to reroute in a dream to avoid King Herod and protect baby Jesus. In case we are heading the wrong way filled with dangers, I pray in the name of Jesus that God will grant us the discerning spirit to be able to know when to reroute for the sake of safety, in the name of Jesus. Amen!

It is written: *"When they heard the king, they departed; and behold, the star which they had seen in the east went before them, till it came and stood over where the young Child was. When they saw the star, they rejoiced with exceedingly great joy. And when they had come into the house, they saw the young Child with Mary His mother, and fell down and worshiped Him. And when they had opened their treasures, they presented gifts to Him: gold, frankincense, and myrrh.* **THEN, BEING DIVINELY WARNED IN A DREAM** *that they should not return to Herod, they departed for their own country another way"* (Matthew 2:7-12 NKJV; emphasis added). What a wicked world we live in! It is written:

"The heart is deceitful above all things, and desperately wicked; Who can know it" (Jeremiah 17:9 NKJV). The heart is not something one can open up to see what is inside of it. ONLY God can see EVERYTHING. I pray that we and our "wise men" will ALWAYS find another way of escape from those planning to harm us and that we will learn to listen to the divine warnings and not be too wise in our own eyes, in the mighty name of Jesus. Amen!

The "Nebuchadnezzars" in Your Life

Who are the "Nebuchadnezzars" in your life who have ordered that you be thrown into a "fiery furnace?" May the good Lord surprise them. I pray that God will be there to guide and protect you; you will not be burnt, and you will come out shining like gold, in the name of Jesus.

It is written: *"Then Nebuchadnezzar was full of fury, and the expression on his face changed toward Shadrach, Meshach, and Abednego. He spoke and commanded that they heat the furnace seven times more than it was usually heated. And he commanded certain mighty men of valor who were in his army to bind Shadrach, Meshach, and Abednego, and cast them into the burning fiery furnace. Then these men were bound in their coats, their trousers, their turbans, and their other garments, and were cast into the midst of the burning fiery furnace. Therefore, because the king's command was urgent, and the furnace exceedingly hot, the flame of the fire killed those men who took up*

Shadrach, Meshach, and Abednego. And these three men, Shadrach, Meshach, and Abednego, fell down bound into the midst of the burning fiery furnace" (Daniel 3:19-23 NKJV).

The "Nebuchadnezzars" in your family (from, mother's, father's or in-law's sides), the ones at work, unfriendly friends all around you will not have power over you, no matter how enraged they get at you, in the name of Jesus. They might have given their commandments for the "furnace" to be heated up more than normal. They may think they have you bound and ready to throw you into the "fire." May the God of Shadrach, Meshach and Abednego be with you. May He turn any form of "fiery furnace" in your life into an air conditioning room and grant you peace in the midst of the "storm," in the name of Jesus. Very soon, your "Nebuchadnezzar" will acknowledge the presence of God in your life, in the name of Jesus. The Lord will break the chains and set you free from any form of bondage, in the name of Jesus. You are coming out with your "coats," your "trousers," "turbans," "garments," and ALL God has blessed you with that you were bound in while you were thrown in the "fire." You are not coming out the same but refined, purified, renewed and filled with the glory of God. He will multiply your blessings, in the mighty name of Jesus. Amen!

It is written: *"Then King Nebuchadnezzar was astonished; and he rose in haste and spoke, saying to his counselors, "Did we not cast three men bound into the midst of the fire?" They answered and said to the king, "True, O king. "Look!" he answered, "I see four men loose, walking in the midst of the fire; and they are not hurt, and the form of the fourth is like the Son of God. Then Nebuchadnezzar went near the mouth of the burning fiery furnace and spoke, saying, "Shadrach, Meshach, and Abednego, servants of the Most High God, come out, and come here." Then Shadrach, Meshach, and Abednego came from the midst of the fire. And the satraps, administrators, governors, and the king's counselors gathered together, and they saw these men on whose bodies the fire had no power; the hair of their head was not singed nor were their garments affected, and the smell of fire was not on them"* (Daniel 3:24-27 NKJV).

May the good Lord use the situation you are going through to show His power to your "Nebuchadnezzars." May the good Lord surprise all those who have gathered to mock/ridicule you or treat you like a nobody. They will gather and be AMAZED to the point that they will have no choice but to praise the Lord with you. The Lord will use your story to win souls for His kingdom, in the name of Jesus. Your testimony will make them bow in TOTAL adoration to the Lord. The Lord Himself will call you out of the "fire." It will not have power over you. You will NOT get "hurt/burnt." I pray you will not experience the "smell of fire" on you in any way. May your mess be turned into victorious messages, in the mighty name of Jesus. Amen!

It is written: *"Nebuchadnezzar spoke, saying, "Blessed be the God of Shadrach, Meshach, and Abednego, who sent His angel and delivered His servants who trusted in Him, and they have frustrated the king's word, and yielded their bodies, that they should not serve nor worship any god except their own God! Therefore, I make a decree that any people, nation, or language which speaks anything amiss against the God of Shadrach, Meshach, and Abednego shall be cut in pieces, and their houses shall be made an ash heap; because there is no other God who can deliver like this." Then the king promoted Shadrach, Meshach, and Abednego in the province of Babylon"* (Daniel 3:28-30 NKJV). May God turn the plans of the enemy toward you or your loved ones into blessings. May you be promoted and celebrated. May your testimonies be full, in the mighty name of Jesus. Amen!

ARE YOU FEELING OLD AND YOU THINK TIME IS AGAINST YOU?

Old age, terminal illness and some forms of disabilities may make people get anxious, depressed or plan to die before death comes. We don't have any power over these concerns but to keep on trusting God, the Author and Finisher of our faith. God promised that He will be with us even to our old age. It is written: *"Even to your old age, I am He, and even to gray hairs I will carry you! I have made, and I will bear; Even I will carry, and will deliver you"* (Isaiah 46:4 The NKJV). It is writing: *"Therefore, I say to you, do not worry about your life, what you will eat or what you will drink; nor about your body, what you will put on. Is not life more than food and the body more than clothing? Look at the birds of the air, for they neither sow nor reap nor gather into barns; yet your heavenly Father feeds them. Are you not of more value than they? Which of you by worrying can add one cubit to his stature?" "So why do you worry about clothing? Consider the lilies of the field, how they grow: they neither toil nor spin; and yet I say to you that even Solomon in all his glory was not arrayed like one of these. Now if God so clothes the grass of the field, which today is, and tomorrow is thrown into the oven, will He not much more clothe you, O you of little faith?" "Therefore, do not worry, saying, 'What shall we eat?' or 'What shall we drink?' or 'What shall we wear? For after*

265

all these things the Gentiles seek. For your heavenly Father knows that you need all these things. But seek first the kingdom of God and His righteousness, and all these things shall be added to you. Therefore, do not worry about tomorrow, for tomorrow will worry about its own things. Sufficient for the day is its own trouble" (Matthew 6:25-34 NKJV NKJV). Our God is faithful! It is written: "I have been young, and now am old; Yet I have not seen the righteous forsaken, nor his descendants begging bread" (Psalm 37:25 NKJV). God will take care of you. Continue to abide under His "wings." By His grace, you will not go begging for food, and you will not be put to shame, in the mighty name of Jesus. Amen!

"God Will Take Care of You" By Civilla D. Martin (1904)

1. Be not dismayed whate'er betide,
   God will take care of you;
   Beneath His wings of love abide,
   God will take care of you.

Refrain
God will take care of you,
Through every day, o'er all the way;
He will take care of you,
God will take care of you.

266

2. Through days of toil when heart doth fail,
      God will take care of you;
  When dangers fierce your path assail,
      God will take care of you.

  3. All you may need He will provide,
      God will take care of you;
  Nothing you ask will be denied,
      God will take care of you.

  4. No matter what may be the test,
      God will take care of you;
  Lean, weary one, upon His breast,
      God will take care of you.

YOU DON'T NEED THE PAIN

"What a friend we have in Jesus, ALL our sins and griefs to bear, Oh, what peace we often forfeit, Oh, what needless pain we bear, all because we do not carry everything to God in prayer." If you know this beautiful song by Joseph M. Scriven, sing it and if you don't know it, read the lyrics and ask yourself these questions: What needless pain am I bearing that is forfeiting my peace? I pray that the God of peace will step into ALL forms of "boats" of worry, anxiety, depression or whatever the problem may be and calm the storm, take away your worries, anxiety and depression, in the name of Jesus. Amen!

Song of Meditation "What A Friend We Have in Jesus"
Lyrics by Joseph Medlicott. Scriven **(1855)**
1. What a friend we have in Jesus,
All our sins and griefs to bear!
What a privilege to carry
Everything to God in prayer!
Oh, what peace we often forfeit,
Oh, what needless pain we bear,
All because we do not carry
Everything to God in prayer!

2. Have we trials and temptations?

Is there trouble anywhere?

We should never be discouraged—

Take it to the Lord in prayer.

Can we find a friend so faithful,

Who will all our sorrows share?

Jesus knows our every weakness;

Take it to the Lord in prayer.

3. Are we weak and heavy-laden?

Cumbered with a load of care?

Precious Savior, still our refuge—

Take it to the Lord in prayer.

Do thy friends despise, forsake thee?

Take it to the Lord in prayer!

In His arms He'll take and shield thee,

Thou wilt find a solace there.

Encouraging Bible Verses

"Therefore, we do not lose heart. Even though our outward man is perishing, yet the inward man is being renewed day by day" (2 Corinthians 4:16 NKJV).

"Moses was one hundred and twenty years old when he died. His eyes were not dim nor his natural vigor diminished" (Deuteronomy 34:7 NKJV).

269

"Wisdom is with aged men, and with length of days, understanding" (Job 12:12 NKJV).

"Do not cast me away when I am old; do not forsake me when my strength is gone" (Psalm 71:9 NIV).

"You will come to the grave in full vigor like sheaves gathered in season" (Job 5:26 NIV).

"The eyes of the LORD are on the righteous, and His ears are open to their cry" (Psalm 34:15 NKJV).

"But those who wait on the LORD, shall renew their strength; They shall mount up with wings like eagles, they shall run and not be weary, they shall walk and not faint" (Isaiah 40:31 NKJV).

"Have I not commanded you? Be strong and of good courage; do not be afraid, nor be dismayed, for the LORD your God is with you wherever you go" (Joshua 1:9 NKJV).

"Peace I leave with you, my peace I give to you; not as the world gives do I give to you. Let not your heart be troubled, neither let it be afraid (John 14:27 NKJV).

"God is our refuge and strength, a very present help in trouble. Therefore, we will not fear, even though the earth be removed, and though the mountains be carried into the midst of the sea; Though its waters roar and be troubled, though the mountains shake with its swelling. Selah" (Psalm 46:1-3 NKJV).

"I will lift up my eyes to the hills. From whence comes my help? My help comes from the LORD, who made heaven and earth. He will not allow your foot to be moved; He who keeps you will not slumber. Behold, He who keeps Israel shall neither slumber nor sleep. The LORD is your keeper; The LORD is your shade at your right hand. The sun shall not strike you by day, nor the moon by night. The LORD shall preserve you from all evil;

He shall preserve your soul. The LORD shall preserve your going out and your coming in from this time forth, and even forevermore" (Psalm 121 NKJV).

Take off the veil and let the king of glory adorn you with His robe of glory. Come to the King of kings for abundant blessing. Let the greatest physician lay His healing hands on you and make you whole. Is it financial issues? Invite Jehovah Nissi into your endeavors and let him bless you. Say this to yourself, your spouse, children, grandchildren, other family members and all your loved ones who are on your prayer list.

"What then shall we say to these things? If God is for us, who can be against us? He who did not spare His own Son, but delivered Him up for us all, how shall He not with Him also freely give us all things? Who shall bring a charge against God's elect? It is God who justifies. Who is he who condemns? It is Christ who died, and furthermore is also risen, who is even at the right hand of God, who also makes intercession for us. Who shall separate us from the love of Christ? Shall tribulation, or distress, or persecution, or famine, or nakedness, or peril, or sword? As it is written: "For Your sake we are killed all day long; We are accounted as sheep for the slaughter" Yet in all these things we are more than conquerors through Him who loved us "
(Romans 8:31-37 NKJV).

Song of Meditation "Through it All" By Andréa Crouch

ANTIDOTES FOR ANXIETY, DEPRESSION AND CARES OF THIS WORLD –REFILL

Welcome to the "pharmacy" of God's Holy word! I tell you, we can never have enough of it. Moreover, we cannot overdose on it either. Another interesting thing about the word of God is that it is new every time one reads it – new interpretations and insights are experienced. Feel free to take as much as you want, anywhere, anytime. For refill, there are so many in the Holy book (Bible). May the spirit of God be with you and take away your worries/anxiety, feeling of guilt, sorrows, pains, depression and ALL the negative emotions. I pray that joy, sound health/mind and God's blessings be yours as you read His words, in the mighty name of Jesus. Amen!

"And do not be conformed to this world, but be transformed by the renewing of your mind, that you may prove what is that good and acceptable and perfect will of God" (Romans 12:2 NKJV).

"Keep your heart with all diligence, for out of it spring the issues of life" (Proverbs 4:23 NKJV).

273

"Who Himself bore our sins in His own body on the tree, that we, having died to sins, might live for righteousness—by whose stripes you were healed" (1 Peter 2:24 NKJV).

"For God so loved the world that He gave His only begotten Son, that whoever believes in Him should not perish but have everlasting life" (John 3:16 NKJV).

"But God demonstrates His own love toward us, in that while we were still sinners, Christ died for us" (Romans 5:8 NKJV).

"For the wages of sin is death, but the gift of God is eternal life in Christ Jesus our Lord" (Romans 6:23 NKJV).

"Be sober, be vigilant; because your adversary the devil walks about like a roaring lion, seeking whom he may devour. Resist him, steadfast in the faith, knowing that the same sufferings are experienced by your brotherhood in the world"
(1 Peter 5:8-9 NKJV).

"But those who wait on the LORD shall renew their strength; They shall mount up with wings like eagles, they shall run and not be weary, they shall walk and not faint" (Isaiah 40:31 NKJV).

"No temptation has overtaken you except such as is common to man; but God is faithful, who will not allow you to be tempted beyond what you are able, but with the temptation will also make the way of escape, that you may be able to bear it"
(1 Corinthians 10:13 NKJV).

"But may the God of all grace, who called us to His eternal glory by Christ Jesus, after you have suffered a while, perfect, establish, strengthen, and settle you" (1 Peter 5:10 NKJV).

"You will not need to fight in this battle. Position yourselves, stand still and see the salvation of the LORD, who is with you, O Judah and Jerusalem!' Do not fear or be dismayed; tomorrow go out against them, for the LORD is with you"
(2 Chronicles 20:17 NKJV).

"And seeing the multitudes, He went up on a mountain, and when He was seated His disciples came to Him. Then He opened His mouth and taught them, saying: "Blessed are the poor in spirit, for theirs is the kingdom of heaven. Blessed are those who mourn, for they shall be comforted. Blessed are the meek, for they shall inherit the earth" (Matthew 5:1-5 NKJV).

"Casting all your care upon Him, for He cares for you"
(1 Peter 5:7 NKJV).

"Behold, God is my salvation, I will trust and not be afraid; For YAH, the LORD, is my strength and song; He also has become my salvation" (Isaiah 12:2 NKJV).

"He will fulfill the desire of those who fear Him; He also will hear their cry and save them" (Psalm 145:19 NKJV).

"Finally, brethren, whatever things are true, whatever things are noble, whatever things are just, whatever things are pure, whatever things are lovely, whatever things are of good report, if

275

there is any virtue and if there is anything praiseworthy—meditate on these things" (Philippians 4:8 NKJV).

The "patch" form is available below. It can be on the fridge, in your bedroom, war room any room or any were. There are sample and blank forms. Use as needed. Be blessed:

PUT YOUR NAME IN THE BLANKS AND APPLY THE BLESSINGS TO YOURSELF. Use this as an example:

But now, thus says the LORD, who created me Oh: Bosede Apata And He who formed you, Oh: Bosede Apata *"Fear not, for I have redeemed you; I have called you by your name; You are Mine. When you pass through the waters, I will be with you; And through the rivers, they shall not overflow you. When you walk through the fire, you shall not be burned, nor shall the flame scorch you. For I am the LORD your God, the Holy One of Israel, your Savior; I gave Egypt for your ransom, Ethiopia and Seba in your place. Since you were precious in My sight, you have been honored, and I have loved you; Therefore, I will give men for you, and people for your life. Fear not, for I am with you; I will bring your descendants from the east, and gather you from the west"* (Isaiah 43:1-5 NKJV).

Here Is A Blank One for You

"But now, thus says the LORD, who created me, Oh: _____

And He who formed you, Oh: _____ *"Fear not, for I have*

redeemed you; I have called you by your name; You are Mine.

When you pass through the waters, I will be with you; And

through the rivers, they shall not overflow you. When you walk

through the fire, you shall not be burned, nor shall the flame

scorch you. For I am the LORD your God, the Holy One of Israel,

your Savior; I gave Egypt for your ransom, Ethiopia and Seba in

your place. Since you were precious in My sight.

You have been honored, and I have loved you; Therefore, I will

give men for you and people for your life. Fear not, for I am with

you; I will bring your descendants from the east and gather you

from the west" (Isaiah 43:1-5 NKJV)

I hope you have been touched. Remain Blessed.

Song of Meditation "He Touched Me" By Bill Gaither

HAVE ATTITUDE OF GRATITUDE

"If we know how to think, we will know how to thank." Looking around, there will always be one thing to thank God for. The fact that we are alive is enough to praise His holy name. Many have died. We are too blessed to be stressed. May God teach us how to count our blessings and to set our priorities right. God's love, favor and grace toward our families and us are too numerous for us to allow anything/anyone to steal our joy. These are some of the reasons I cannot afford to allow stress to destroy me, and you shouldn't either: Jesus died for me (Romans 5:8). He said in His book, I am fearfully and wonderfully made (Psalm 139:14). He promised to fight my battles, and He told me that I should not worry about ANYTHING. I just have to be silent (Exodus 14:14). It is written: *"The LORD is my shepherd; I shall not want. He makes me to lie down in green pastures; He leads me beside the still waters. He restores my soul; He leads me in the paths of righteousness, for His name's sake. Yea, though I walk through the valley of the shadow of death, I will fear no evil; For You are with me; Your rod and Your staff, they comfort me. You prepare a table before me in the presence of my enemies; You anoint my head with oil; My cup runs over. **SURELY** goodness and mercy shall follow me, all the days of my life; And I will dwell in the house of the LORD, forever"* (Psalm 23 NKJV; emphasis added). All I want to say is

278

THANK YOU, LORD! God has been so good to me. The Lord is AWESOME!

Prayer

Father, I praise you for ALL the unmerited favors. I know you are still working on me. Kindly forgive me, Lord, for being anxious for no reason. Take the anxiety away, Father, and grant me the grace to fully commit my ways unto you. I love you, Lord. Accept my thanks and praises, in the name of Jesus. Amen!

HE WILL HIDE ME

As we travel through the "wilderness journey," I pray that God will continue to hide and protect us from all harms and dangers, in the name of Jesus. It is written, *"For He shall give His angels charge over you, to keep you in all your ways. In their hands they shall bear you up, lest you dash your foot against a stone. You shall tread upon the lion and the cobra, the young lion and the serpent you shall trample underfoot. He shall call upon Me, and I will answer him; I will be with him in trouble; I will deliver him and honor him. With long life I will satisfy him, and show him My salvation"* (Psalms 91:11-13, 15-16 NKJV). With the unseen/seen forces surrounding us, He kept us. In the midst of COVID and challenges of life, God remains faithful! May He continue to preserve our lives and deliver us from every evil work, in the name of Jesus, Amen! It is written: *"And the Lord will deliver me from every evil work and preserve me for His heavenly kingdom. To Him be glory forever and ever. Amen!"* (II Timothy 4:18 NKJV). May we find refuge, under the shadow of God's hand, throughout the rest of our lives. May God answer our prayers as we call upon Him and grant us long life, in the mighty name of Jesus. Amen!

Song of Meditation "When the Storms of Life Are Raging,"
By Mary E. Servoss (1881)

1. When the storms of life are raging,

    Tempests wild on sea and land,

    I will seek a place of refuge

    In the shadow of God's hand.

Refrain

He will hide me, He will hide me,

Where no harm can e'er betide me;

He will hide me, safely hide me,

In the shadow of His hand.

2. Though He may send some affliction,

    'Twill but make me long for home;

    For in love and not in anger,

    All His chastenings will come.

3. Enemies may strive to injure,

    Satan all his arts employ;

    He will turn what seems to harm me

    Into everlasting joy.

4. So, while here the cross I'm bearing,

    Meeting storms and billows wild,

    Jesus for my soul is caring,

    Naught can harm His Father's child.

281

LEAVE THE BURDEN WITH THE LORD

Due to the challenges of life and the UNNECESSARY burdens we have been carrying around, we may be feeling as if we are about to be moved to the edge and about to fall. God will not allow this to happen, in the name of Jesus. May the good Lord continue to sustain us and keep us from falling. It is written: *"And He said to me, "My grace is sufficient for you, for My strength is made perfect in weakness." Therefore, most gladly I will rather boast in my infirmities, that the power of Christ may rest upon me"* (II Corinthians 12:9) God will NEVER fail. *"Cast your burden on the LORD, And He shall sustain you; He shall never permit the righteous to be moved"* (Psalms 55:22 NKJV). May He grant us the grace to cast our "burdens" on Him and leave them there, in the mighty name of Jesus. Amen!

Song of meditation "Leave it There" By Charles Albert Tindley (1916)

1. If the world from you withhold of its silver and its gold,

And you have to get along with meager fare,

Just remember, in His Word, how He feeds the little bird—

Take your burden to the Lord and leave it there.

Refrain

Leave it there, leave it there,

Take your burden to the Lord and leave it there;

If you trust and never doubt, He will surely bring you out—

Take your burden to the Lord and leave it there.

2. If your body suffers pain and your health you can't regain,

And your soul is almost sinking in despair,

Jesus knows the pain you feel, He can save and He can heal—

Take your burden to the Lord and leave it there.

3. When your enemies assail, and your heart begins to fail,

Don't forget that God in Heaven answers prayer;

He will make a way for you and will lead you safely through—

Take your burden to the Lord and leave it there.

4. When your youthful days are gone and old age is stealing on,

And your body bends beneath the weight of care;

He will never leave you then, He'll go with you to the end—

Take your burden to the Lord and leave it there.

GOD'S PLAN FOR OUR LIVES

The thief does not come except to steal, kill and destroy. Jesus came that WE MAY HAVE LIFE IN ABUNDANCE (John 10:10). God's plans for us are of good, not evil. First, we must acknowledge that we need Him, and He will replenish ALL that the enemy has stolen from us.

Before thinking of killing ourselves, let us remember Jesus on the cross—all the agony He passed through for you and me to be saved. The plan did not end on the cross; he has gone to prepare a place for us. He is coming back to take us home to be with Him (John 14:3).

We are at the "airport" waiting for our "PILOT" JESUS to come. REMEMBER, waiting on a flight is not easy. No matter how long we wait at the airport for our flights, we don't carry our comforters and pillows to get too comfortable. We try our best to make sure we don't miss our flights. May we not be found wanting when our "Pilot" (JESUS) comes, in His holy name. Amen! It is written: *"He who is coming will come and will not tarry"* (Hebrews 10:37). He is coming victorious, in the name of Jesus. "Soon and very soon, we are going to see the king!" Our Lord, Redeemer and Savior. Hold the fort brother/sister in the Lord. We are overcomers, in the name of Jesus. We don't have to kill ourselves. Jesus died, but now He lives. Because He lives, we can face the challenges through His grace. We serve a mighty God, who can move mountains. He is awesome. He is able to hide/protect us from all that is disturbing us, be it "rain," "sunshine, "mountains" or "valley." He is able to see us through, in the mighty name of Jesus. Amen!

DON'T GET TOO COMFORTABLE

As Christians, we know we can't get too comfortable here on earth. We are pilgrims, just passing through. Jesus has gone to prepare a place for us. He promised to come back and take us home with Him. He is FAITHFUL! He is coming back as He has promised. It is written: *"Let not your heart be troubled; you believe in God, believe also in Me. In My Father's house are many mansions; if it were not so, I would have told you. I go to prepare a place for you. And if I go and prepare a place for you, I will come again and receive you to Myself; that where I am, there you may be also"* (John 14:1-3 NKJV). There is no place like home! There will be no more sorrow, no more pain of any kind. There will be no fear of thieves, kidnapers, terrorists, COVID or any form of plague. The Lord will take away the fear of anything that will steal our peace, in the name of Jesus. Amen! May God help us to lay our treasures up in heaven. It is written: *"Do not lay up for yourselves treasures on earth, where moth and rust destroy and where thieves break in and steal; but lay up for yourselves treasures in heaven, where neither moth nor rust destroys and where thieves do not break in and steal. For where your treasure is, there your heart will be also"* (Matthew 6:19-21 NKJV). Kindly look for me when you get there. May we all reign ETERNALLY with Him, in the mighty name of Jesus. Amen!

Signs of the times are EVERYWHERE! Watch and pray. The world is not the same anymore. Many saints are sleeping in the Lord. They don't need to worry about the challenges of this world anymore. Some of us will be alive when He comes. It is written: *"Behold, I tell you a mystery: We shall not all sleep, but we shall all be changed"* (1 Corinthians 15:51 NKJV). While we are waiting patiently for His coming, He wants us to occupy until He comes. We will continue to do what we are supposed to do as we travel along the "wilderness journeys." May God shed His light/glory on our ways as we walk with Him, trusting and obeying His words. May we allow Him to lead us, and may we be willing to do His will for the rest of our lives, in the name of Jesus. Amen!

Song of Meditation "When We Walk with the Lord" By John H. Sammis (1887)

1. When we walk with the Lord

in the light of his word,

what a glory he sheds on our way!

While we do His good will,

He abides with us still,

and with all who will trust and obey.

Refrain

Trust and obey, for there's no other way

to be happy in Jesus, but to trust and obey.

287

2. Not a burden we bear,

not a sorrow we share,

but our toil he doth richly repay;

not a grief or a loss,

not a frown or a cross,

but is blest if we trust and obey.

3. But we never can prove

the delights of his love

until all on the altar we lay;

for the favor he shows,

for the joy He bestows,

are for them who will trust and obey.

4. Then in fellowship sweet

we will sit at his feet,

or we'll walk by his side in the way;

what he says we will do,

where he sends we will go;

never fear, only trust and obey.

COUNT DOWN

Condolences to the families who have lost their family members on the "battlefield." May God console you and wipe your tears away, in the name of Jesus. Amen! When Jesus comes to take us home, we will be able to reunite with our loved ones. Hold on, brother/sister. "It won't be long." It is written: *"In a moment, in the twinkling of an eye, at the last trumpet. For the trumpet will sound, and the dead will be raised incorruptible, and we shall be changed. For this corruptible must put on incorruption, and this mortal must put on immortality. So, when this corruptible has put on incorruption, and this mortal has put on immortality, then shall be brought to pass the saying that is written: "Death is swallowed up in victory." "O Death, where is your sting? O Hades, where is your victory?" The sting of death is sin, and the strength of sin is the law. But thanks be to God, who gives us the victory through our Lord Jesus Christ Therefore, my beloved brethren, be steadfast, immovable, always abounding in the work of the Lord, knowing that your labor is not in vain in the Lord"* (1 Corinthians 15:52-58 NKJV).

Song of Meditation "O There'll Be Joy When The Work is Done" By F. E. Belden

1. Oh, there'll be joy when the work is done,

Joy when the reapers gather home,

Bringing the sheaves at set of sun

To the New Jerusalem.

Refrain

Joy, joy, there'll be joy by and by,

Joy, joy, where the joys never die;

Joy, joy, joy, for the day draweth nigh

When the workers gather home.

2. Sweet are the songs that we hope to sing,

Grateful the thanks our hearts shall bring,

Praising forever Christ our King

In the New Jerusalem.

3. Pure are the joys that await us there,

Many the golden mansions fair;

Jesus Himself doth them prepare,

In the New Jerusalem.

I WILL WEAR A CROWN

Darling brother/sister in the Lord, just imagine the joy of a happy life that awaits us with our Savior. There is NOTHING comparable to what He has prepared for us. But as it is written: *"Eye has not seen, nor ear heard, nor have entered into the heart of man the things which God has prepared for those who love Him"* (1 Corinthians 2:9 NKJV). The Lord does not want us to be distracted. It is written: *"Behold, I am coming quickly! Hold fast what you have, that no one may take your crown"* (Revelation 3:11 NKJV). May God help us to endure to the end. It is written: *"Blessed is the man who endures temptation; for when he has been approved, he will receive the crown of life which the Lord has promised to those who love Him"* (James 1:12 NKJV). Brother/sister in the Lord, imagine when we FINALLY see Jesus, walking the streets of gold, where there will be no more sickness, no more death, we will not have to worry about anything ANYMORE. HALLELUJAH! Just imagine the joy that will fill our hearts. May we be amongst those who will sing and shout songs of victory!" I pray that you and I will be recipients of the crown and robe of glory, in the mighty name of Jesus. Amen. Any time you feel down, just remember that Jesus loves and cares for you.

Song of Meditation "Sing the Wondrous Love of Jesus" By E.E. Hewitt (1898)

1. Sing the wondrous love of Jesus,

   sing his mercy and his grace;

in the mansions bright and blessed

   he'll prepare for us a place.

Refrain:

When we all get to heaven,

what a day of rejoicing that will be!

When we all see Jesus

we'll sing and shout the victory.

2. While we walk the pilgrim pathway

   clouds will overspread the sky,

but when traveling days are over,

   not a shadow, not a sigh.

3. Let us then be true and faithful,

   trusting, serving every day;

just one glimpse of Him in glory

   will the toils of life repay.

4. Onward to the prize before us!

   Soon His beauty we'll behold;

Soon the pearly gates will open-

We shall tread the streets of Gold.

IN CONCLUSION, I SAY: ABIDE WITH ME, LORD!

We are thanking God for His faithfulness, for the forgiveness of our sins. We are casting ALL our cares on Him, trusting that He will abide with us FOREVER. He will ALWAYS be our guide throughout our "wilderness journey." With Him by our sides, we will not fall by the wayside. Together, we will make it to glory land, in the name of Jesus. Darling brother/sister in the Lord, I am trusting God that; You have been blessed reading this book. Thank you once again for your support. I pray that the peace of God will continue to abide with you FOREVER, in the mighty name of Jesus. It is written: *"So, the ransomed of the LORD shall return, and come to Zion with singing, With everlasting joy on their heads. They shall obtain joy and gladness; Sorrow and sighing shall flee away"* (Isaiah 51:11 NKJV). May God take away your sorrow, fill your mouth with songs of praise. May everlasting joy be yours and your loved ones, in the name of Jesus. I pray that God will not allow the enemy to have power over you. May He take away the depression, anxiety and all the other negative things keeping you down, in the name of Jesus. It is written: *"Arise, shine; For your light has come! And the glory of the LORD is risen upon you"* (Isaiah 60:1 NKJV). Your light has come," in the name of Jesus! With these blessings, I pray: *"The LORD bless you and keep you; The LORD make His face shine upon you, and be gracious to you;*

293

The LORD lift up His countenance upon you, and give you peace"
(Numbers 6:24-26 NKJV). I pray for sunshine in your soul today.
NEVER give up. ALWAYS. RISE AND SHINE, in the mighty
and precious name of Jesus. Amen!

Song of Meditation "There Is Sunshine in My Soul Today"

Eliza Edmunds Hewitt

1. There is sunshine in my soul today,
More glorious and bright
Than glows in any earthly sky,
For Jesus is my light.

Chorus
O there's sunshine, (O there's sunshine in my soul,)
blessed sunshine, (blessed sunshine in my soul,)
When the peaceful, happy moments roll
When Jesus shows His smiling face,
There is sunshine in my soul.

2. There is music in my soul today,
A carol to my King;
And Jesus, listening, can hear
The songs I cannot sing.

3. There is music in my soul today,
For when my Lord is near
The dove of peace sings in my heart,
The flowers of grace appear.

4. There is gladness in my soul today,
And hope and praise and love
For blessings which He gives me now,
For joys "laid up" above.

Prayer

"Forever, O Lord, your word is settled in heaven." Thank you, Father, for your goodness and mercies over us. Thank you once again for the opportunity given to be able to write this book and for blessing my sister/brother with the messages in it. I pray that the blessings will be permanent, in the name of Jesus.

Forgive us for allowing the cares of this world to get us down. Teach us to take this life one day at a time. Remind us that your coming is very near, and you will put an end to the challenges of this world. Until then, Father, help our hearts to keep on singing your praises. Keep us strong and firm to the end. Help us not to lose focus. May we not be like the "foolish virgins" but like the wise virgins, keeping our lamps burning bright to the end. More than anything, Father, we pray that at the end of our journey here on earth, you count us worthy of your glorious kingdom, in the mighty name of Jesus. Amen! SHALOM!